ENGLISH NEWS WRITING

English News Writing

A Guide for Journalists Who Use English as a Second Language

Bryce T. McIntyre

The Chinese University Press

English News Writing: A Guide for Journalists Who Use English as a Second Language

By Bryce T. McIntyre

ISBN: 978–962–201–731–3

First edition 1996
Second printing 2009

THE CHINESE UNIVERSITY PRESS
The Chinese University of Hong Kong
SHA TIN, N.T., HONG KONG
Fax: +852 2603 6692
+852 2603 7355
E-mail: cup@cuhk.edu.hk
Web-site: www.chineseupress.com

Printed in Hong Kong

For Jill and Jodi —
lost, but never forgotten

Contents

Preface

English is a giant. Of some 2,700 languages in the world, English is a megalanguage, spoken by about 1 billion people. The only other language in this class is Chinese, which may be spoken by another 100 million or so — assuming, of course, that its hundreds of dialects comprise a single language.

English is the mother tongue of six nations, and it is an official or semi-official second language in at least 20 others — Zambia, Nigeria, Singapore, Kenya, Tanzania, to name a handful. More people speak English in India — and more English language dictionaries are sold there — than in Great Britain.

English wiped out its competition in the last hundred years. Like a muscular, overgrown teenager, English rudely brushed aside Spanish and French as the *lingua franca* of international commerce and diplomacy. On this score, Esperanto and Interlingua, which were created exclusively for this esteemed role, will be lucky to get one-liners when the final history of language is written. How all this happened — whether it is a result of "Coca-colonialism", or whether English is, as some say, a lingual sea fed by all the tributaries on earth and washing up on every shore — are questions for pundits, not me.

"All I know," as the popular American humorist Will Rogers often said, "is what I read in the newspapers." From them it is clear that thousands of journalists use English as a second language. Giant English language wire services hire local personnel to staff foreign bureaus. And there are outstanding English language newspapers in many nations where English is a second language — the *Jerusalem Post*, the *Bangkok Post*, the *Indonesian Observer* (Jakarta), *Media Asia* (Singapore), the *New Straits Times* (Kuala

Lumpur), the *Times of India* (New Dehli and Bombay), the *Philippine Daily Express* (Manila), and the *South China Morning Post* (Hong Kong), to name a few.

These facts attest to the need for a journalism handbook for journalists who use English as a second language. Most of these journalists reside in some 45 Commonwealth nations.

The need for this book became evident when I began teaching journalism at The Chinese University of Hong Kong. Although I had taught journalism for almost a decade at several American universities, I realized from the day I walked into a classroom in Hong Kong that I faced a new set of issues, and this book addresses those issues.

A special feature of this book is my *42 Rules of Thumb*. The purpose is, in part, to personalize my view of the most important rules of news reporting and writing. I borrowed the idea for this from Strunk and White, a long-time favorite about writing — and a book that every writer should read.[1]

Aside from the rules of thumb, this book differs from other journalism references in a number of ways. For one, I lapsed into first and second person in a few places — again, to personalize my message. I have mulled over this issue since 1988, when I began work on *Advanced Newsgathering*. My instincts as a journalist were to keep myself in the background. My instincts as an educator were to develop a personal relationship with the reader.

Finally I decided, why not? This is a book based largely on my personal experiences as a journalist and educator. Although in Chapter 2 I strongly urge writers to avoid first and second person, I make limited use of it here — for pedagogical reasons only.

Another difference is that this book provides a few examples of what the writer should *not* do as well as what the writer *should* do. Common mistakes identified in this book came from students. These problems face beginning writers everywhere.

This book differs from other journalism references also in its focus on *writing* as opposed to *reporting*. By **reporting**, I mean newsgathering. Newsgathering techniques vary widely across countries. In some nations, for example, journalists may be required to submit questions in writing to

[1] William Strunk, Jr., and E. B. White, *The Elements of Style* (New York: The Macmillan Company, 1959).

government officials before interviews will be granted. This is unthinkable elsewhere.

Although the focus of this book is on writing, reporting is still treated here. This is made possible by the existence of certain universals. There is little difference between the ways journalists cover speeches and public lectures in different countries, for example. The same applies to some interviewing techniques and other subjects.

If there is an advantage to emphasizing writing over reporting, it is that more space can be devoted to journalistic structures — and this is probably of more value to ESL journalists. This is because learning to write is more important than learning about governmental organization. Governmental organization can be learned quickly on the job.

Throughout the book, I faced the ticklish problem of straddling British and American style and usage. This problem was most acute with regard to newspaper jargon. In an anonymous review of the preliminary manuscript by someone that I took to be an English newspaperman working in Hong Kong, I was criticized for my use of the word *lede* (also spelled *lead*) to mean *the first paragraph of a news story.* "This is not used on UK newspapers," wrote the reviewer, "and hence rarely found in Hong Kong newsrooms, where 'intro' is usual...." Frankly, I disagree. But, assuming that he is correct just for the sake of discussion, the term nevertheless *is* used by the world's three largest wire services, the Associated Press, United Press International — even the UK-based Reuter. In fact, Reuter defines *lead*, but not *intro*, in its *International Style Guide*. Now, I cannot debate my critics on a point-by-point basis. My purpose here is to merely illustrate the problem I faced with regard to the jargon of this business. My solution has been to follow wire service usage with regard to newspaper jargon and to point out differences in usage whenever a major term is introduced to the reader.

This book differs from others also in not having a separate chapter on ethics. In this book, a few basic ethical principles are nevertheless established in the first chapter, but they are presented without discussion or elaboration. My reason for this is twofold. First, I believe that ethical principles should be taken up in depth at a more advanced level of a journalist's training. Second, I believe that ethical principles should take into account local customs. In any event, I appended two codes of ethics for reference — one from the United States and one from Hong Kong. I strongly urge readers to review these after reading Chapter 1.

Another difference between this book and other journalism books is its lack of treatments of newsroom organization, newspaper production and operations, and computer techniques in writing and editing.

The way these subjects are treated in most journalism references presupposes the existence of computer-intensive work environments. These are not typical of lesser developed nations. Also, computer systems vary across news organizations, and it is pointless to teach them all — or even one of them at the expense of the others.

Besides, I believe that learning to write is more important than learning about organizations and machines. In this sense, I am a purist. The concepts of writing are the same whether the student is writing with a computer, with a typewriter, or with a pencil stub on the inside of a matchbook cover — a condition I have resorted to myself on a few occasions.

A few overly pedantic scholars will disagree with me on this, but I believe that the process of writing is independent of the machinery used to produce it. Mastery of technique, not machinery, will bring success to the aspiring writer, and I hope the following pages provide some inspiration in this regard.

Bryce T. McIntyre
Hong Kong
1 December 1995

42 Rules of Thumb for Good Writing

Elementary Rules of News Reporting

Elementary Rules of Lead Writing

Elementary Rules of News Writing

1

The Basics

Some people think the word ***news*** comes from the points of the compass — north, east, west, south. It doesn't. *News* is the plural of *new*, the noun. This is an insight into what news is.

News is new — timely, fresh, immediate. A ferry sinks and five passengers die. The journalist does not wait for the ferry company to file its reports with local authorities. "Journalist", after all, is from the French words *jour*, which means day, and *journal*, which means daily record: The *journalist* is a person who keeps a daily record. Events are reported the same day. In only a few days, the event becomes history — old, stale, dusty. At least in the eyes of the journalist.

For this reason, one attribute of news is *timeliness.*

Now, news must be more than timely. It must be relevant — relevant to the audience. Events inside a community are more relevant to its residents than are events outside. A ferry that sinks in a town's harbour creates more interest locally than it does halfway around the globe. It will see extensive coverage in local papers. It may merit only a ***brief*** — sometimes called a ***news brief*** — in distant newspapers, one or two paragraphs.

For this reason, a second attribute of news is *proximity.*

If 300 passengers die in a sinking ferry, then it gets greater coverage, locally and elsewhere. This is true for most news events: When large numbers of people are affected, the news is more compelling.

For this reason, a third attribute of news is *magnitude.*

A lot of news deals with power struggles. Examples include major corporations that compete with each other in the same market; prime ministers who argue about policy with parliaments; labour unions that negotiate with businessmen for better wages. Although large numbers of people may not be affected, the details of the fight are of great interest to newspaper readers.

For this reason, a fourth attribute of news is *conflict.*

Many news stories focus on strange phenomena. A 10-foot Burma python is found in the yard of a local member of parliament; a 13-year-old boy commits suicide because he is not doing well at school; a woman gives birth to quintuplets. Such events are newsworthy because they are bizarre and unusual.

For this reason, a fifth attribute of news is *oddness.*

If you were playing a guitar for some of your friends at your residence, and you suddenly dropped dead of a heart attack, the news media probably would not write a story about the event. However, if Paul McCartney were playing a guitar for some of his friends and he dropped dead of a heart attack, the news media would write a river of news about the event. This would be newsworthly only because Paul McCartney is a famous person. An event involving an ordinary citizen that seems commonplace may become a major event if it involves a prominent person.

For this reason, a sixth attribute of news is *prominence.*

In summary, the main attributes of news are timeliness, proximity, magnitude, conflict, oddness and prominence. When a journalist is assessing a potential news event for its newsworthiness, these are the criteria that come into play.

Types of News

News has many faces. ***Hard news*** is news that must be reported, like the examples just cited. Hard news compels journalists to action; there is no quibbling about its newsworthiness. The resignation of a prime minister is hard news; a nationwide referendum is hard news.

Spot news is hard news that happens suddenly and unexpectedly, on the spot. Preparing for it in advance is almost impossible. The crash of a jumbo jet is spot news; an armed robbery of a jewellery store is spot news.

Journalists cover some news events for several days. The crash of a jumbo jet on Monday will be followed by a series of stories about the crash on Tuesday, Wednesday, Thursday and Friday. After the initial crash article, or ***story***, the additional stories will be about investigations, and they will include speculation about the causes. An eyewitness might surface with an interesting account. Such stories are called ***follow-ups***, and they focus on the most recent developments. In writing follow-ups, journalists say they are ***following a story***. Editors ask reporters, "Will you follow that?" When there are no new developments, journalists stop following the story.

There is a kind of hard news that compels journalists to follow it for weeks or months. It continues indefinitely, taking on a life of its own. Each day brings another major development, another surprise. Such stories are called ***continuing big stories*** or ***running stories***. The collapse of the Soviet bloc was a continuing big story. The eruption of Mount Pinatubo near Manila was a continuing big story. Bosnia is a continuing big story.

Stories like these often cause journalists to pause and reflect about the significance of events. They do the same when pondering the complex issues of international treaties and trade agreements. One result may be the ***news analysis***. The news analysis is somewhat interpretative. Its goal is to render the complex, simple. It attempts to explain things to readers.

There are days when a major event transpires, and journalists cannot wait for all the facts to come in. A prime minister is mortally wounded by a sniper. News bulletins appear immediately on the radio and television. A special afternoon edition of the newspaper is planned, an ***extra***. The situation changes hour by hour. Police close off the central district of the city; the prime minister succumbs; a successor is installed in office. This is a ***developing story*** or a ***breaking story***.

So far, all the kinds of stories identified here have been hard news. What about a story based on an interview with a filmmaker? Or one about a Christmas tree sales in Penang? These do not compel journalists to action, and they certainly are not hard news. Stories about filmmakers and Christmas tree sales are therefore called ***soft news***. Soft news has a timeless quality about it, meaning that it can be printed almost any day, within a reasonable period of time. And if it were not printed at all, nobody would miss it.

Some stories seem to have no other purpose than to describe people and places. After an attempted *coup d'état* in the Soviet Union, a story appeared with the headline, "Life for Muscovites Shuffles On, Much as Before the Coup." A laconic Moscow barber said, "People's hair kept growing during the coup, and they kept coming in for haircuts." This is soft news, but it's also colourful, so it may be called a ***colour story***.

Colour stories often run beside hard news. Their purpose is to flesh out the stark details of a major news event. They supplement a longer, related story. A story, or ***piece***, that runs beside a longer, related story is called a ***sidebar***. The longer story is the ***main piece***.

Colour stories are feature stories. A ***feature story***, or ***feature***, is often written in a distinctive style, and it provides an emotional, colourful, humorous or personal slant to a subject. A feature story about a hard news event is called a ***news feature***.

Features take many forms. Included are interviews, personality profiles, how-to articles, and self-help pieces. When a journalist finds himself caught in the throes of a news event, sometimes his personal reactions are written in the first person and published as a ***reporter's notebook***, another type of news feature.

Another is the ***retrospective***. This is a look back at a news event. It may be written one year later or 50 years later, like a retrospective on the opening days of the war with Japan.

There are days when several similar events occur within a short period. Example: It's the New Year in Hong Kong and, in unrelated events, two children are blinded by fireworks, one loses a finger and two experience broken eardrums. A story that begins, "Five children were seriously injured Monday in separate incidents involving fireworks," is a ***roundup***. A round-up pulls together separate news events with common elements, reporting them all in a single news story. British journalists use the expression ***leadall*** or ***wrap-up***.[2] Finally, there is the so-called ***investigative story***. This is *an in-depth investigation into a matter in which information is being deliberately concealed or withheld from the journalist.* The secrecy usually stems from fears of prosecution for criminal wrongdoing or bad publicity. Investigative reporting requires detailed understanding of complex legal issues, a heightened sensitivity to detail, good sources, and strong reporting

[2] According to *Reuters International Style Guide*, there are two kinds of leadall in British usage. One is the kind that is defined above. The other is a separate story that summarizes several related stories, all of which are presented in their entirety under separate datelines.

and writing skills. For these reasons, investigative reporters are often viewed as the ultimate professionals in journalism.

Journalistic Ethics

Ethics are universally situational in journalism: There is no single ethical principle that is absolute. No point in mincing words: Some journalists will lie, cheat and steal to get a good news story, especially if they believe they are acting for the common good. On the other hand, there are journalists who will ***spike*** or ***kill*** a good story — that is, they will cancel it — to avoid embarrassing a private citizen. In any case, deceptions by journalists are commonplace. Censure for unethical conduct is rare and usually of little consequence.

Codes of ethics promulgated by journalists' associations are commonplace, but they are widely ignored. In spite of this, there are a few principles that are widely received. In this text, they comprise the first eight basic rules of thumb for news reporting. The first rule concerns coverage of people in life-threatening situations.

Journalists are routinely dispatched to cover events in which people are in danger. These people may be trapped in burning buildings, taken hostage by gunmen, caught in a turgid river.

Although the journalist is there to gather news, his first responsibility is to protect the lives of others. This gives us Rule No. 1.

Rule No. 1:
Protect individual lives and safety first.

Protection of individual lives and safety takes precedence over newsgathering. Journalists who witness people in danger desist from newsgathering and provide assistance, if this is feasible.

The next rule concerns bribery. The president of the Hong Kong Journalists Association said that Chinese journalists often accept money from Chinese businessmen and community leaders in mainland China in exchange for publishing nice stories about them and their activities. This is highly unethical. Journalists should not accept payment from outside sources in exchange for writing news about special interests. They should not accept gifts, free travel, or special treatment from news sources.

Rule No. 2:
Do not accept money from sources in exchange for writing news.

Another unethical practice that concerns the exchange of money is the journalist's paying sources for news. This is called ***chequebook journalism***, and it is practised in both Great Britain and the United States. To engage in this practice opens you to public criticism in the journalistic community, so it is best to avoid it.

Rule No. 3:
Do not pay sources for information.

Very naive sources will sometimes ask you how much money you will give them in exchange for an interview. Merely tell them that this is not done, that it is indeed unethical. Most of them will allow you to interview them anyway.

One small exception to this rule is payment to cover routine costs of reproduction of documents and postage, for example, if your source incurs some costs in providing you with information.

The next rule concerns a practice that is all too widespread — writing "news" that actually promotes the interests of your newspaper's advertisers. This can be very misleading to readers, who assume you are objective. If you do this, you have violated their confidence in you as a journalist.

Some newspapers such as the *South China Morning Post* in Hong Kong have a special department closely related to the news department that does nothing but write "special reports" for advertising supplements. In my view, this practice comes very close to breaching this important ethical principle, and it is acceptable only under the following conditions: (1) news staff reporters are in no way involved in writing the copy; (2) news staff photographers are in no way involved in taking the photographs; (3) the department is under the supervision of the advertising director, not the editor; and (4) all material written and published by the department is clearly identifiable as advertising content, either by use of different typefaces and layouts, or by prominent display of the phrase "Advertising Supplement".

Rule No. 4:
Do not write promotional "news" about advertisers.

In a well run newspaper office, the advertising department will be widely separated from the news department — usually on a different floor — so there is no influence from the advertising department on the news decisions of editors. When I was a managing editor, I had two very strict rules about this: (1) no advertising personnel were allowed in the newsroom; (2) no advertising personnel were permitted to suggest ideas for news stories to my reporters. All such suggestions had to be put to me, and if I thought there was a genuine story about an advertiser, then I would assign a reporter to cover it.

As you can infer from this, advertisers are sometimes newsworthy. They usually want you to publish news about management promotions and retirements, new factories and big contracts, new retail outlets.... All of these might be legitimate news for the business section of your newspaper, but news about advertisers should be subjected to the same criteria as news about nonadvertisers.

The next rule concerns news about yourself. You might think you are not newsworthy; however, when you work as a journalist, you sometimes find yourself deeply involved in a news event. This has happened to me a few times. Once I was physically assaulted by two prominent legislators who threatened to murder me. I beat them off and escaped. Fortunately, there were many witnesses, but I was the only journalist present.

Rule No. 5:
Do not write news about yourself or your family.

I knew this was a major news story — prominent members of the community do not behave this way — but I did not know how to report it. My account would not be seen as objective. My managing editor asked me to write him a memorandum containing everything I could remember about the event, including background that might have led up to it. Then he telephoned the two men and asked them for their versions of the story. They not only corroborated everything I said, but also apologized publicly. My boss also interviewed some witnesses who confirmed the details.

My managing editor himself then wrote the story and ran it on Page 1. It caused a major political scandal that continued for weeks and included formal investigations. The story was picked up and run as front page news by all of our major competitors.

So, you cannot predict that you never will be involved in a news event; indeed, I suspect you will be. When it happens, turn the story over to someone else.

Most good newspapers have a basic rule that news about any staff member is subjected to the same criteria as news about members of the general public. The flip side of this policy is that you cannot expect your news organization to spike a story about your involvement in a wrong-doing. If you kill a pedestrian while driving an automobile under the influence of alcohol, then your newspaper should handle the story as it would for anyone else.

Of course, news about your family should be subject to the same criteria — and for the same reasons.

News about you and your family obviously involves you in a conflict of interest. Conflict of interest is a broader question that deserves separate treatment, however, so I have created a separate rule for it.

I strongly believe that journalists should not be active in political parties. I also believe that you should not talk about your own political views with your sources.

If you live in a democratic society, then you have a social obligation to take an interest in political matters and to vote; however, if you wear your politics on your sleeve, then you will inevitably be perceived as partisan. You will be denied access to information; some of your sources will dry up; and all of your news will be seen as tainted.

Rule No. 6:
Avoid potential conflicts of interest.

You might think this will never happen to you because you are not very interested in politics. Chances are very high, however, that after a few years of covering issues in your community, you will be invited to participate in panel discussions and policy making bodies because of your expertise, your knowledge of the issues. You will be invited to speak to clubs and professional organizations. You will feel honoured by such requests, but you should reject them if you sense any possible compromise of your objectivity.

Another way to preserve your objectivity is to present both sides of an issue, even if you strongly disagree with one of them. Many times when I was reporting news I thought people were lying to me in interviews, but I was obligated to report their statements anyway, just in fairness. Indeed, one of my greatest frustrations as a journalist was feeling obligated to report information that I did not believe myself.

When faced with such a predicament, I would seek out an impeccable source who would express a countervailing opinion, and I would report that opinion as well and let the reader decide who was lying.

Rule No. 7:
Make a reasonable effort to be accurate and fair.

A common source of unfairness in journalism arises when one prominent member of the community makes unkind or incriminating statements about another member of the community. Individuals who make unsubstantiated charges against another member of the community should not be quoted anonymously. Victims of such allegations should be given an opportunity to respond to the charges.

Note that Rule No. 7 states that you should make a *reasonable* effort to be accurate and fair. I chose this word with great care. If Source A says that Source B is embezzling money; if Source A is willing to go on the record publicly with this allegation; if you confirm Source A's allegations, either with documents or with Source C; if you try many times to reach Source B by telephone and pager and fax and he seems to be avoiding you; then you should go ahead and write the story, adding, "Source B could not be reached for comment on the allegations."

You see, we cannot ***sit on a story*** merely because someone will not talk to us. If we did that, we never would get any good stories.

There are times when people caught in nasty situations will agree to be interviewed, but they will preface their remarks with something like this: "I'll agree to speak to you, but only if you let me approve the story before it is published."

Rule No. 8:
Do not yield stories to sources for approval prior to publication.

This is a ridiculous request. Why do we have editors? Besides, *you're* the journalist — *you* decide what's newsworthy, not your sources. The journalist, the editors and the publisher are the final judges about what is published in the newspaper. You should reject any such request outright.

Again, I chose my words carefully. Notice that I said you should not yield stories for *approval* prior to publication. This is because some journalists, as a courtesy, will provide a copy of story to a source prior to publication *merely for informational purposes only.*

Another practice is to telephone a source and read quotes from the source back to him as a means of verifying their accuracy. This is done in extremely sensitive situations when the precise wording is important.

Objectivity

Objectivity is impartiality, disinterest, fairness, balance, neutrality, accuracy. It is a shared value in the worldwide community of journalists. Nevertheless, most members of this community would agree that no one is truly objective.

This is easily demonstrated. The significance that journalists find in events is not an inherent attribute of the events; it is brought to the events by the journalists, who bear elaborate social constructions of reality in their heads. These mental constructions are heuristics whose purpose is to interpret events and find meaning in them. Thus, critics accuse journalists of inventing reality.

Rule No. 9:
Be objective.

If this is true, where does that leave us? It can be said at least that objectivity is a professional standard, one that is never quite reached.

The standard is loosely met in a straightforward way, with a criterion called ***verification***. This is what is meant by verification: *A journalistic* *account of a news event — that is, a news story — is considered objective if details of the account can be verified independently by other observers.*

This is an empirical approach to news, and it sounds almost scientific. This is because scientists and journalists have much in common: They both observe cultural and physical phenomena; they both describe their observations to audiences; and they both rely on independent observers to establish their impartiality. This last process, which journalists call verification, is called *inter-observer agreement* or *replication* by scientists.

The principal differences between journalists and scientists lie in their methods and in their goals. Scientists investigate specific phenomena as a means to reach generalizations, which they call theories, paradigms, and laws. Journalists report specific observations day after day as an end in itself.

Indeed, they often are criticized for this, for not drawing conclusions and for not painting a broader picture. Perhaps it is good that they don't, because this gives the scientists something to do.

News Jargon

An important part of learning a new profession is learning its language. In this sense, the profession of journalism is no different from others. We already have learned a lot of new terms. Here are a few more to complete the lesson.

When journalists write, they produce ***copy***. A technical definition would read something like this: *Copy* is *typewritten material destined for publication.* Words on paper are sometimes called ***hard copy***. A computer file is ***soft copy***. In this context, *copy* has no plural form: "Where's Friday's copy?" thus means "Where are all the stories that were written Friday?" You should not say "Friday's copies."

Similar terms are ***matter*** and ***material***. ***Typewritten matter*** or ***material*** is copy produced on a typewriter. ***Typeset matter*** is copy that has been set in type. Typesetting formerly was done on Linotype, Intertype, or Monotype machines that cast type with molten lead. Their output was called *hot type*, and the machines themselves were called *hot metal* machines. Other names for them were *linecasters* or *typecasters*. Today typesetting is more commonly done with computers. Hence the term *cold type* is used.

Sometimes journalists write copy before events occur. When a head of state becomes deathly ill and retires to his bed, journalists don't wait until he dies to begin writing the ***obituary***, or *death notice*. The ***obit***, at it sometimes is known, is written in advance and stored in a file. It is ***advance copy*** or ***A-matter***, for ***advance matter***.

A special type of advance is the ***curtainraiser***. This is a long-ish, analytical piece on a major event that is about to take place — an election, for example — and it normally is ***filed***, or given to the editors, several days ahead of the event. Curtainraisers are deliberately *interpretative*, a concept central to the news analysis, defined above.

A-matter may be written on many other occasions. A journalist who works Monday through Friday every week may be asked to write copy for a Sunday edition. If so, he or she will produce a ***weekend advance***. Another example: Public opinion polls are commonplace in some countries, so the outcomes of elections may be known beforehand. In such cases, journalists may write A-matter summarizing the main issues in the elections. Then they ***put a new top on*** the story — that is, they write a new beginning paragraph or paragraphs — after all the votes have been counted.

The matter that follows the opening paragraph or paragraphs of a story is known as the ***body*** of the story. The body is composed of paragraphs, or ***grafs***, in American newsrooms. Elsewhere, paragraphs may be known as ***pars*** or ***paras***.

The beginning of a story is called the ***lead***, but in American newsrooms, the word is sometimes spelled *lede* in order to distinguish the pronunciation from that for the word *lead*, meaning the metal, which was commonly used in the printing process in former days. Usually the lead is a single sentence. This single sentence is usually the first paragraph of the story.

A news story may be referred to as a ***piece***. A synonym is ***item***. In fact, some old-fashioned newspapers were called *itemizers*, and the term is still used in some places.

A related term, one found in book and magazine publishing, is manuscript. Like the word copy, ***manuscript*** means typewritten material destined for publication. The difference is that a manuscript is quite long. Magazine articles and books are much longer than newspaper articles.

More specifically, a 55,000-word novel in English would be considered rather short by today's standards, and magazine articles tend to range from 2,000 to 3,500 words. Newspaper stories, on the other hand, are long-ish if they run more than about 750 words. It is trendy today for newspaper articles to be longer than they have been in the past, so you will see longer articles from time to time. One long article in this book that illustrates this trend is *taki*, on Page 127.

Copy Preparation

The process journalists use to prepare copy for their editors is called ***copy preparation***. The technique of copy preparation varies for different media. Newspapers, magazines, radio stations, and wire services have their own conventions. The same may be said for the film and television industries, and for book publishers.

There are some standard practices, however. For magazine and book publishers, where a single piece of copy is normally referred to as a *manuscript*, the text is almost always typewritten and double-spaced. Even a manuscript that is written on a computer, when output as hard copy, will be printed in a conventional typewriter face such as Courier and double-spaced. This is because book and magazine editors like the *portability* of printed copies — they can write notes on them, photocopy them, share them with other editors.

In the newspaper business, however, the short production cycle does not allow for this leisurely approach to handling copy. There, hard copy is single-spaced because it is edited directly on computers within the organization in which it was produced, and it is handled by only one or two people before it is set in type.

In printing jargon, a typeface is known as a ***font***.

A conventional typewriter font is ***nonproportional*** — that is, all the letters are the same width, so an "l", for example, takes up the same amount of space as a "W" on a line of typewritten text. Also, the font will have 10 characters per inch. In computer programmes that offer alternative fonts, the abbreviation for "characters per inch" is *cpi*. *A nonproportional typewriter font with 10 cpi is referred to as pica. A nonproportional typewriter font with 12 cpi is referred to as elite*. Editors prefer pica to elite because it is bigger.

Typewritten matter produced for books and magazines should be written on standard A4 size paper using a line length of 65 characters. On a typewriter, for example, if the left margin is set at 10 and the right margin

Figure 1.1 Proportional and Nonproportional Fonts

```
This font is Courier. The widths of all the characters are
the same. Ten l's are the same width of 10 capital m's. This
is why it is called a nonproportional font.

     llllllllll                      1111111111
     tttttttttt                      2222222222
     MMMMMMMMMM                      3333333333
```

This font is Helvetica. The characters have different widths, making a more pleasing design. Notice that numerals have the same widths in both fonts; this makes it easier for editors to line up numbers in columns when creating numerical tables.

llllllllll	1111111111
tttttttttt	2222222222
MMMMMMMMMM	3333333333

---

at 75, then there will be 65 spaces in between. The average English word is about six letters long, so 65 characters will provide just enough space for an average of 10 words per line.

When copy is produced in this manner, editors can quickly determine the length of a piece in words by counting the number of lines and multiplying by 10.

If the copy is centered on the page, then the right and left margins are about one inch, or 2.5 centimetres. Top and bottom margins should be the same, with the exception of the top margin of the first page. Editors need some space to write notes, so writers usually leave the top third of the first page blank, with the exception of their names, dates and other pertinent information.

If the above guidelines are followed for copy preparation, then the typical page will have 250 words on it, and this also will allow editors to determine how long the article is: Every four pages is 1,000 words. This would be long-ish for a newspaper story and short for a magazine article. In magazines, very long stories — more than 5,000 words, say — are often run in pieces in successive editions, or ***serialized***. Extra long newspaper articles are run as ***series*** also.

When writing for magazines, authors write their own titles for their articles, but newspaper reporters do not do this. At newspapers, copy editors write the titles — they are called ***headlines*** or ***heads*** at newspapers — because they have to fit a certain amount of space that is a function of the design of the newspaper. And this design function is outside the purview of the newspaper reporter.

This text is written for journalists, so the focus here will be on preparing copy for newspapers. Each news story is given a short name, and this name is called a ***slug***. An equivalent term on a computer is ***filename***, and filenames are used interchangeably with slugs at some newspapers. Like filenames, slugs usually are one word, and each one should be unique on any given day. Also, slugs are not capitalized, even when derived from proper nouns. An editor who asks, "Where is that *smuggle* story that Rodney was working on?" is referring to a story called *smuggle*. There should be only one story by this name in the newspaper on this day in order to avoid confusion. In a sense, the slug is a moniker, a nickname, a one-word "handle" that facilitates communication and aids in the production process.

Some slugs are ***standing slugs*** or ***master slugs***, meaning they are used every day. A reporter who covers a legislature on a daily basis will file at least one main story about that body each day, and his slug may be *xgr*, a common American journalistic abbreviation for "legislature". A main *xgr* story may be accompanied by another one by the same reporter that focuses on a lesser issue — approval of an appointment of a bureaucrat, for example, in which case the slug might be something like *xgr-appoint.*

If the legislature story needs a complete rewrite, then its revision might be called *xgr-rew.*

There are times when journalists file stories before all the facts are in. This may be the case, for example, in a story about an exploding volcano written for a newspaper that has more than one edition in a single day: In a case like this, there would be one story for the first edition and another story for the second edition.

If the body of the story can ***stand*** — that is, run in the second edition without changes — then only the lead may be revised. The original story would be called *volcano* and the first revision of the lead would be called *volcano 1st lead.* This may seem confusing because it actually is the second lead; the way I remember it is to think of the *1st lead* as the 1st *new lead.*

Sometimes journalists write ***inserts*** for breaking stories, and these are slugged with the word "insert", as in *volcano-insert,* with instructions on where to make the insertion. The instructions usually look something like this: "sub third graf The names of the deadxxxxxxxnot released, pickup fourth graf The scenexxxxxxxthat area". This is journalistic shorthand for "The text that follows should be used as a substitute for the third paragraph of the story called volcano. The third paragraph begins with 'The names of the' and ends with 'not released'. After substituting the third paragraph with this material, resume the story with the fourth paragraph of the original volcano story, which begins 'The scene' … ."

A ***take*** is one page of typewritten copy, in the traditional sense as outlined above. Nowadays, the term is used by wire services to mean a text file with 200 to 300 words in it. A 750-word story, a typical length for a wire service dispatch, is usually comprised of three takes.

The second take is usually referred to as the ***first add***, meaning ***first additional take***. The nomenclature may seem confusing, but it is widely used and should be remembered.

As mentioned on the previous page, the title of a newspaper story is referred to as a ***headline*** or ***head***. The credit line that identifies the writer and his position in the news organization — for example, "By David Hoffman, Washington Post Service" — is called a ***byline*** because it begins with the word "by". If the story itself begins with the name of the city in which the news event originated, then this line is known as the ***dateline***. It looks like this: *MANILA — Mount Pinatubo erupted Monday for the third time this year, causing thousands to flee….* Datelines get their name from the fact that, in former times, the date of the news event followed the name of the city; however, in contemporary practice, most news is reported the same day, so the convention has been eliminated. Datelines are written in all capital letters, and the name of the country may follow in caps and lowercase if the city is not well-known. Because the dates are rarely provided nowadays, datelines are called ***placelines*** at some newspapers.

As mentioned above, reporters for the daily press do not write headlines or give themselves bylines. Writing headlines is a duty of editors, not writers, and this is due partly to the fact that the headline is a design element, and it must be written with a view toward design. As for the byline, editors usually dole these out as rewards for well crafted items, and, as rewards, they should not be given by writers to themselves.

Art is any illustrative material that accompanies a news item. It most likely is not "art" in the usual sense of the word, but a photograph of a news event. It also could be graphs or sketches. In slugging stories with art, journalists indicate this with a notation like *volcano w/art.* A story from a wire service would include a notation such as *laserphoto,* a reference to the laser technology used in reproduction.

Decisions about art are usually made by a photo editor, who assigns photographers to work with reporters and then reviews photos as they are processed later in the day. At a small newspaper, the decisions would be made by another editor with additional duties.

The Newspaper Paragraph

The newspaper paragraph doesn't have the same form as the paragraph used in traditional essay-style writing, or *composition.* Classical composition form will be reviewed briefly here merely to provide a contrast. The traditional essay has three parts — the introduction, the body and the conclusion. The *introduction* is one or two paragraphs that establish the *thesis,* the main idea of the essay. The *body* of the essay is a series of paragraphs that break the thesis into parts, each paragraph beginning with a *topic sentence* that identified the main point of the paragraph. The *conclusion* is usually a one-paragraph summary.

Here is an example of a body paragraph beginning with a topic sentence:

> Built on the Acropolis overlooking the city of Athens in the fifth century B.C., the Parthenon is an excellent example of Greek architecture. It was a temple of the gods and was very important to the people. Although at first glance its structure seems to be perfect, on closer examination it becomes clear that it is a static, two-dimensional object. As long as you stand in the center of any of its four sides to look at it, its form will appear to be perfect. The strong Doric columns seem to be equally spaced, one next to another, along all four of its sides. But if you take a step to the right or left, the Parthenon's symmetry is destroyed.[3]

---

[3] Laurie G. Kirszner and Stephen R. Mandell, *Patterns for College Writing: A Rhetorical Reader and Guide*, 2nd edition (New York: St. Martin's Press, 1983).

Notice that this paragraph is six sentences long and is highly unified. In sharp contrast to this, however, *the newspaper paragraph has no topic sentence, it is usually only one or two sentences long, and it infrequently exceeds three sentences.*

Here is an example of newspaper paragraph style:

> Witnesses said that three men, two with handguns and one with a knife, entered Wong Yee Jewellery about 12:25 p.m.
>
> Two customers and three staff members were in the store at the time, and the robbers demanded that everyone lie on the floor.
>
> All of the men wore dark clothing, gloves and training shoes, and they spoke to one another in Mandarin rather than Cantonese, according to one witness.
>
> One of them used the butt of his pistol to smash three display cases containing precious stones and gold items. These were scooped up and put into a cloth bag carried by one of the men.
>
> Meanwhile, Mr. Wong Iam Ching, the proprietor of the store, pressed a silent alarm that alerted police.

In the above example, note that *all but one of the paragraphs are only one sentence long*. Although this rule does not apply to long analytical pieces, beginning writers should establish the habit of striking the Enter key on their computers immediately after striking the full stop.

Here is a rule of thumb:

Rule No. 24:
Strive for a paragraph length of 1 to 1.5 sentences.

It takes time to become comfortable with this rule; however, once the rule becomes ingrained, your work will look highly professional.

Sentence Length

Writers tend to be more intellectual than the populace as a whole. This lets them craft long, compound-complex sentences that may be brilliantly executed, but are as tough as walnuts.

The average length of sentences in English has shrunk dramatically over the centuries. In Elizabethan writing, the average sentence length was 45 words. The Victorian sentence was 29. The contemporary sentence is less than 20. According to research done by Prof. Wayne Danielson at the University of Texas, the average sentence length of contemporary American novels is slightly less than 15 words.

Research by United Press International and the Associated Press has clearly established that shorter sentences are easier to understand than longer ones. UPI distributed a table to remind writers of the value of short sentences. It appears in Figure 1.2 below.

Figure 1.2 Sentence Length and Readability

8 words or less	Very easy to read
11 words	Easy to read
14 words	Fairly easy to read
17 words	Standard
21 words	Fairly difficult to read
25 words	Difficult to read
29 words	Very difficult to read

Rule No. 25:
Strive for a sentence length of 17 words or less.

For a good example of the power of short sentences, read carefully the story *taki* in Chapter 8.

News Cycles

Morning newspapers are known as ***a.m. papers***, or just ***a.m.s***. Afternoon papers are ***p.m. papers***, or ***p.m.s***.

Whether an a.m. or a p.m., a newspaper is reissued as an entirely different edition each day. The production process operates on a 24-hour cycle. This gives rise to the terms a.m. cycle and p.m. cycle.

Wire services sell news both to a.m. and to p.m. newspapers, so they have to transmit two entirely separate sets of news stories each day. For the morning newspapers, there will be an ***a.m. cycle*** that begins about between noon and 2 p.m., local time, and ends 12 hours later. The ***p.m. cycle*** begins between midnight and 2 a.m., local time.

The timing of events in the stories for the two cycles may differ. For example, a story on the p.m. cycle that begins "French President Francois Mitterand Tuesday will meet...," might be rewritten as "French President Francois Mitterand today meets ..." for the a.m. cycle.

Sometimes news is written in such a way that it can be utilized in both cycles, or ***b.c***.

Beats and Desks

This book is not about news organizations, so staffing and production cannot be discussed at length here. But something should be said about the journalist's beat, because it is such an important concept.

A ***beat*** is *the area or activity the journalist is responsible for covering.* So, in every news organization there is a *police beat*, a *government beat*, and so on. If a journalist publishes a story before his rivals from other news organizations, he *beats the competition*. Sometimes we say he *got a scoop*.

Beats are organized around desks. ***Desks*** are *departments in a news organization.* Most major news organizations have a *metro desk*, an *international desk*, a *sports desk*, a *business desk*, and so on. In Hong Kong, most newspapers have a *China desk*. People in charge of desks usually have the title of *editor* — *business editor*, *sports editor* — although *chief reporter* is commonly used in some British style organizations. Young, inexperienced reporters are sometimes called ***cub reporters***, which is an old-fashioned American term that shows up from time to time, or ***cadets***, which is common at British newspapers. ***Junior reporter*** is also used at some organizations.

Normally, when a journalist is first learning a new beat, he or she is taken around by the chief reporter or editor and introduced to the principal figures on the beat. For the police beat, for example, the journalist should be personally acquainted with the chief investigators of all the major *squads*, or departments, on the police force — homicide, burglary, robbery, traffic, fraud — not to mention the police force's main media representative, or public affairs officer, and possibly even the police chief himself.

Normally it takes a long time — several months, in fact — for journalists to establish themselves on new beats. One gimmick used by reporters to ingratiate themselves among principal figures on a new beat is the puff piece. A ***puff piece*** is *a relatively shallow, inconsequential article that calls attention to personal achievements of a news source*. Sometimes an editor might say to a reporter, "Why don't you *puff him up a little*?", meaning "Why don't you *write a puff piece*?"

One example might be an uncritical personality profile. Such a profile gives face to the interviewee. Later, when the journalist needs confidential information for a story, the interviewee may be more cooperative.

This is one of the tricks of the trade.

2

Style, Usage and Idiom

One of the best things about English is its rich vocabulary. The *Oxford English Dictionary*, a terminal authority on the subject, lists about 500,000 words, and it has been said that an equal number remain uncatalogued. By comparison, French has fewer than 100,000 words, and German about 185,000.

Facing a potential pool of some 1 million words, writers are fortunate that 90 percent of writing in English is done with 1,000 basic words. This makes life easy for writers as long as they use words they know. It also makes life miserable if they don't.

This leads to an axiom about writing: Writers should use words they know. Many beginners don't understand this simple rule. Beginning writers love to hunt for new words. They often overreach. Thumbing through a dictionary or thesaurus in search of new words is an occupational hazard for writers. This is especially true for writers whose English is a second language.

In one recent reporting assignment, I received student papers with the following words: *communitarian, ethnization, ethnicization, thornbird, meritocracy, commodification, bathetic, punctilious, actualize* and *geocultural.* I had never seen some of these words before. And my 2,500-page copy of the second, unabridged edition of *The Random House Dictionary of the English Language* has definitions for about 315,000 words, but some of those words were not in my dictionary.

I call these "fancy words". I am not impressed by them. Fancy words like "bathetic" and "punctilious" are better off in dictionaries than in newspapers. Writers should keep dictionaries on their desks, but they should use them only as references. Dictionaries should not be used as shovels for digging up words that are better off dead and buried.

Here's a good rule: *Avoid big words*. Big ones cause

INCOMPREHENSIBILITIES.

The incomprehensible writer is a flop. One of the ways I avoid big words is to count the syllables. A word with four or more syllables makes me raise my eyebrows: Is there a shorter alternative? I ask myself.

Here's another rule: *Avoid old and unusual meanings*. Common words like "instant" have dusty, old meanings that live on forever in dictionaries and ancient prose: "Your letter of the 14th instant here yesterday." This sentence uses "instant" to mean "current month". Now, just because this is in the dictionary does not mean the word can be used this way. The dictionary is not a license to write 400-year-old English.

In sum, writers must pick their words carefully. This issue — the issue of what words to use — is mainly the issue of usage. Usage is using words right. Or correctly. That's what this chapter is mainly about.

But first, a note about writing.

The Writing Process

Now that the basics have been established, it is time to begin writing.

Writing is a process. Scholars divide it into three stages: prewriting, freewriting and rewriting.

Prewriting includes all the work before the writer commits words to paper. Research in the newspaper's ***morgue***, or library, discussions with editors and other journalists, visits to government agencies and interviews with subjects and their acquaintances — all of these activities are part of the prewriting stage.

Freewriting begins the moment the writer puts words on paper. Some journalists type up their notes before they actually begin the first drafts of their stories, and this is freewriting. Other journalists draw up outlines, and this also is freewriting. The first draft of an article is often rough, so it also is part of the freewriting process. It should be noted, however, that daily print journalists work under severe time constraints, so outlining and typing notes usually occur when the story is unusually complex and the journalist has the time for this. In fact, time constraints can be so severe that journalists occasionally dictate their stories over a telephone without even writing them down, leaving the writing to a subeditor.

Rewriting begins when the journalist begins revising freewritten matter — and this is where the writing, *per se*, begins. *The greatest weakness of beginning writers is their failure to recognize the importance of this stage of the writing process*. It is here that the writing is ***polished***, or refined, to professional standards. It is here that the writer executes a clever turn of phrase, incorporates rhythm, finds the perfect metaphor to capture the essence of a locale.

Many of the concerns addressed in this stage of the writing process are concerns with style, usage and idiom. These are taken up next.

Style

The word "style" has a rather narrow meaning in journalism, a meaning that is uncommon in other fields of writing. In other fields of writing, we talk about a writer's "whimsical style" or "transparent style".

Susan Sontag, one of America's leading literary critics, uses the term this way in her discussion of *style* as opposed to *content*:

> Of course, as everyone knows or claims to know, there is no neutral, absolutely transparent style. Sartre has shown, in his excellent review of *The Stranger*, how the celebrated "white style" of Camus' novel — impersonal, expository, lucid, flat — is itself the vehicle of Meursault's image of the world (as made up of absurd, fortuitous moments). What Roland Barthes called "the zero degree of writing" is, precisely by being anti-metaphorical and dehumanized, as selective and artificial as any traditional style of writing. Nevertheless, the notion of a styleless, transparent art is one of the most tenacious fantasies of modern culture. Artists and critics pretend to believe that it is no more possible to get the artifice out of art than it is for a person to lose his personality.[1]

Some critics prefer *form* to *style*, and I shall use the word "form" in order to avoid ambiguity. I had a hidden agenda in choosing Ms Sontag's

---

[1] Susan Sontag, *Against Interpretation* (New York: Dell Publishing Co., 1961).

discussion of form. Aside from its use of the word "style" in the tradition of literary criticism, she uses the phrases white style and zero degree of writing.

In my view, if there is a form that distinguishes newspaper writing from literature, then it might properly be described in the words that Ms Sontag uses — neutral, transparent, white. This is because, in most news, literary devices — humour, irony, contrast — are excluded from the text, which itself is typically little more than a series of facts laid out for the reader in a form most convenient for rapid comprehension. Thus, newspaper writing tends toward *pure exposition*. Journalists, in their haste to get out the hard news, rarely develop their potential as *auteurs*.

Journalists often come under fire for their handling of news events in this way, and journalism students with literary ambitions are dismayed to discover this feature of news writing.

As mentioned at the beginning of this section, the word "style" has a much narrower meaning in journalism. In journalism, ***style*** is a received set of rules for capitalization, spelling, abbreviation, usage and punctuation that provide formal consistency in writing the news.

A short example will make this clear. Notice that all of the following sentences are grammatically correct:

> Mister Nolan has lived at Number 26, Waterloo Road, since December 21, 1991.
>
> Mr Nolan has lived at No 26, Waterloo Road, since 21 December 1991.
>
> Mr. Nolan has lived at No. 26, Waterloo Rd., since Dec. 21, 1991.
>
> Nolan has lived at 26 Waterloo Road since Dec. 21, 1991.

Because all of these are grammatically correct, you might think that any one of them would do in writing a newspaper story. But this is not true: If every journalist used whichever style he preferred, then newspapers would be stylistically inconsistent. Readers might think that newspaper editors did not know what they were doing, and this, in turn, would damage the credibility of the press. Because all of the above are grammatically correct, newspaper editors form committees to study stylistic alternatives in order to reach consensus on which ones are most appropriate for their organizations. Their work results in so-called ***style guides***, which are in wide use throughout the industry.

Generally speaking, newspaper style is dominated by the style of four major international wire services — Reuters, the Associated Press, United Press International, and Agence France Presse, each of which publishes its own style guide. Most major news organizations supplement the wire services' style guides with their own local ***stylebooks***, and one of the journalist's first duties on joining a new organization should be to master the local style.

Usage

Aside from style, one of the most immediate concerns facing the writer is usage. The word "usage" was defined above, but here is a more succinct definition: ***Usage*** is *the selection of words in writing*. There are many issues in usage, including person, clichés, foreign expressions, and slang — not to mention British, as opposed to American, usage.

Person refers to alternative pronouns that indicate whether one is spoken to, spoken about, or speaking. There are three — first person (*I, me, my, mine, we, us, our, ours*), second (*you, your, yours*), and third (*he, she, it, him, her, his, hers, its*). There also are so-called *reflexive* forms in each group — *myself, yourself*, and *himself*, for example.

Rule No. 35:
Do not use first or second person outside direct quotations.

Here is a poor lead from a student. It opens a profile of a traditional Chinese doctor who practises folk medicine:

> I waited for half an hour for a Chinese doctor to turn up at his homey clinic in an old and shabby street near Sheung Wan.

In this example, *I* is first person. It's also the first word of the story. The story is about a Chinese doctor, not about the writer. But the writer has inadvertently placed herself in the foreground and drawn unnecessary attention to herself.

Observe how easy it would have been for the writer to keep herself out of the story:

> The Chinese doctor was half an hour late at his homey clinic in an old, shabby street near Sheung Wan.

If you were a film director, you wouldn't dare stand dead square in front of the camera for the whole film. Don't do it in writing, either.

In avoiding the first person, writers distance themselves from the subject, and this contributes to the perception of an objective reality. This in turn aids in maintaining the writer's *objectivity*. There's more about objectivity in Chapter 1.

Sometimes writers find it absolutely unavoidable to allude to themselves. Even so, there are ways to do this without using the first person. Here's one way to do it, through the third person:

> A survey of those who had babies ... found people had come up with names in a dream, a song and a phone book. Parents are again plucking names from the family tree after years of avoiding it. "In general, the family has been out as a source of names," says C.N. Textor, who tracks name trends as a hobby. "It may be the yuppies' idea of reinventing the wheel." In choosing a baby's name, this reporter bypassed family names that include Precious Lillie, America Hedgepath and Venus Lulu and went with Anna Rose.[2]

Some writers may find the *this-reporter* reference somewhat stilted. Here's another way for the writer to refer to herself, one that is not so stilted:

> WASHINGTON — A young woman called, a publicist: "Taki thought you might want to know what he looks like."
>
> But his photograph is on the book jacket.
>
> "That won't help, I'm afraid."
>
> What will?
>
> "He'll be wearing a blue blazer," she said, then broke into a giggle. "And he's very tan." Gold pinkie ring, macho sport watch, tan infinitum.... Taki wiped some sweat in the Hay-Adams lobby. A five-block dash in the heat had temporarily impaired the power of his charm.[3]

---

[2] *The Asian Wall Street Journal*, Wednesday, 17 July 1991, (Vol. XV, No. 223), pp. 1, 20.

[3] *International Herald Tribune*, Hong Kong edition, Saturday–Sunday, 31 August–1 September 1991, (No. 33,750) p. 20. This story is reproduced in full in Chapter 6, Personality Profiles.

In the above paragraphs, there are two full, direct quotations by the writer: "But his photograph is on the book jacket" and "What will?" The writer cleverly captured her own quotes without resorting to first person. Omitting the quotation marks was her way of signalling that these were her own comments.

Now for the second person. Second person draws the reader into the picture unnecessarily. Following is a paragraph from the work of a beginning writer who has not yet learned this principle:

> Without doubt, the only way to widen your scope is to leave town. Studying abroad becomes a fantasy for many people.

In this paragraph, *your* is second person. It is unnecessary. The story is not about the reader, who may already have a "wide scope" and may already have travelled. The story is about people in general. It is easy to avoid second person. For example, the writer could have written:

> The best way for people to broaden their outlook is to travel abroad.

Another solution might have been this:

> The best way to broaden one's outlook is to travel abroad.

The problem with this solution is that it is too formal for newspaper writing. Newspapers tend to be slightly informal, and *one* is a bit stilted.

Being Precise

Choosing precise words relates to the question of usage. Don't slap down any old word on the page and hope it sticks: Pick your words carefully.

Here is an example of imprecise writing:

> Two fishermen waited in both of the boats tied up at the Marine Police Division dock in Shek O.

How many fishermen were there? Two or four? The sentence would have been clearer if it had been written this way:

> Two fishermen waited in each of the boats tied up at the Marine Police Division dock in Shek O.

Rule No. 26:
Be precise.

If readers want to exercise their imaginations while reading, they can turn to poetry. Meanwhile, it is your duty as a journalist to provide precise information, not to leave the audience guessing about your meaning.

Being Concrete

Words like *very* and *quite* are vague, and they add little to the meaning:

> Mr. Matsushita is a very short man with quite long hair.

How short is "very short" and how long is "quite long"? Don't make your readers guess:

> Mr. Matsushita is 1.3 metres tall and has hair to his shoulders.

Rule No. 27:
Be concrete.

Here's one more:

> The bus ran off the road and rolled down the hill.

Revision:

> The bus smashed through a guard rail and flipped end-over-end down the hill.

Being Concise

Verbiage is excessive words, or wordiness. Wordiness is a problem for all writers, myself included. You should be constantly on the hunt for unnecessary words that you can delete from your stories. In other words, strive for conciseness.

Here is an example of a wordy sentence.

> The Governor visited the site of the blaze in order to assess the damages there for himself.

Revision:

The Governor visited the site.

In the revision, the purpose of the governor's visit should be obvious, and the kind of site should be obvious from the context.

Rule No. 28:
Be concise.

Repetition results in wordiness. It may seem simple to avoid repetition, but it creeps in where you least expect it:

Of all of the fisherman's articles of equipment that he uses, his skiff is the most important to him.

In this sentence, *fisherman's, he, his*, and *him* all refer to the same person.

Revision:

Of all the gear, the skiff is the fisherman's most important.

Identification of People in the News

In discussing the identification of people in the news, editors sometimes use the expression first reference. *First reference* is *the first time that you refer to a person by name in the news.* Likewise, *second reference* is *any reference after the first reference.*

Here is the rule of thumb on identification of news subjects on first reference:

Rule No. 29:
Use a person's full name on first reference.

Aside from the full name, you should include a title, and, if the person represents an organization in the news, then the full name of the organization.

If the person does not represent an organization, the person should be identified with a courtesy title, full name, village or district of the city he lives in, and sometimes his or her age. Here are a few example: *Mr. Kelvin Leung, 18, of Yuen Long ... ; Miss Tsang Pui Ying of Sha Tin, an 18-year-old Form 5 student, said....*

By *full name* I do not necessarily mean every name that a person has. Most Chinese people have three names, and they customarily use all of them, as in "Tsang Pui Ying", above. Westerners, however, typically abbreviate their middle name or omit it altogether. A few merely use initials for their first two names and spell out the last one fully. You should follow their preferred style when identifying them on first reference.

Now, turning to second reference, here is the rule of thumb:

Rule No. 30:
Use a courtesy title and family name on second reference.

Most newspapers use a courtesy title and family name on second reference — *Mr. Li, Ms Chan.* On second reference, you also can use: (1) a pronoun (*he* or *she*); or (2) if the second reference is many paragraphs away from the first reference, then the family name with a clue for the reader about who this person is in the news story (*The Consumer Council's Mr. Chan ...*).

On second reference, you should not refer to a person only by his or her first name: This is amateurish and disrespectful. There are some minor exceptions to these rules, and they will be discussed below.

Minimum Information Required

In writing about people in the news, there is a basic minimum standard that you should meet regarding identification. Here is a basic rule that you should follow when interviewing people: *When interviewing anyone for a news story, you should ask the subject for the following information: (1) full name; (2) proper title (in the case of women, ask which courtesy title they prefer — Miss, Mrs. or Ms); (3) address (home address if not representing an organization in the news); (4) age; (5) occupation; and, if employed, (6) occupational title and name of organization.*

Here are a few examples of proper style: *Mr. Hamish Sullivan, executive director of the Hong Kong Tourist Association ... ; The Hong Kong Tourist Association's executive director, Mr. Hamish Sullivan, reported....*

Note that when you use *the* as I did in the second example, you are required to subordinate the person's name; however, this is not necessary if you omit it. Hence, this also would be correct: *Hong Kong Tourist Association Executive Director Hamish Sullivan reported Monday that....*

In the second example, the man's title is capitalized because it appears before his name and as a personal title. Note also that the courtesy title is dropped.

Other information that readers sometimes expect in the story, especially if the story is a feature story, are marital status, number of children, and miscellaneous personal details such as birthplace, number of brothers and sisters, and so on.

Normally, you would use little of this information in writing the news story. However — and this is a very important basic rule for high-class newswriting — *you should provide enough information about the subject for any casual reader to be able to locate this person, contact him or her, and verify your facts.* Information that is not essential to the identification may be added for colour: *Mr. Cheng, who has been married for 14 years and has two sons....*

Full identification of your subjects keeps you honest, and no one can doubt your objectivity or the source of your facts. If readers have doubts, they can double check the facts themselves.

Exceptional Situations

There are some common exceptions to these rules. For example, the victims of some crimes often are not identified in the news. This is done as a courtesy to the victims, who have suffered enough without having to bear the public humiliation on top of the criminal act itself.

Another exception involves people who are willing to be interviewed, but who are shy about having their names in the press. The journalist should never take this at face value, but should pressure the subject for permission to use his name. If this fails, and if the interview with the subject is really important, then the proper way to identify the person is as follows: *One student, who requested that his name be withheld, expressed anger about the administration's policy*; or, *An anonymous source in the Government Information Service said ...* ; or, *A source who requested anonymity reported Monday that....* This attribution technique is discussed more fully in Chapter 6.

Another technique, and one that should be used only sparingly, is something like this: *Another complaint about the system was filed by "Bill" (not his real name), who....*

For additional information on these conventions, see "Rules of the Road" in Chapter 6.

Occasionally, you will run across news in which people are referred to by their first names. In an interview with Miss Diana Ross, the famous American pop artist, she said, "Just call me Diana." I personally could never do that — it would always have to be *Miss Ross* to me — however, if that is the way she wants to be known, then you should feel free to use her first name on second reference.

Here is a common policy on the use of first names: *Use first names (or given names) on second reference for children under age 16, and for certain celebrities who are seeking to promote an informal persona.* Occasionally, journalists use first names in reference to mentally retarded adults, but this is a questionable practice and is not recommended.

Clichés

Cliché is a French word that refers to a kind of printing plate. A printing plate prints the same image over and over. No matter how exciting an image is originally, it eventually loses its appeal. It becomes worn out.

Today ***cliché*** means *a worn out expression, a platitude*. Unfortunately, there is an abundance of them, and everybody knows too many of them. Clichés sneak into writing like mice in the dark and leave nasty droppings in the text. One cliché will soil an otherwise fine piece. Here is a lead from the *South China Morning Post*:

> Hong Kong, the Jockey Club and River Verdon were big winners at the internationally acclaimed Sha Tin races on Sunday — but a man in his late 20s is smiling all the way to the bank.[4]

---

[4] *South China Morning Post*, vol. 47, no. 349, Tuesday, 17 December 1991, p. 1.

The phrase "smiling all the way to the bank" is a cliché, and it ruins this sentence. Unfortunately, this sentence was the first sentence of the story. And this story was on the front page of the newspaper. The most important impression on the reader is the first one. Make it a good one. Make it brilliant.

Table 2.1 below lists a few clichés. The list is not exhaustive.

Table 2.1 Cliché sampler. Beware, or be square

add insult to injury	long arm of the law
better late than never	make a long story short
beat a hasty retreat	necessity is the mother of invention
busy as a bee	needle in a haystack
cold as ice	nipped in the bud
easier said that done	on the ball
face the music	powers that be
fresh as a daisy	rain cats and dogs
gentle as a lamb	sneaking suspicion
good as gold	stand on your own two feet
hard as a rock	spur of the moment
hit the nail on the head	stand in awe
horse of a different colour	straight from the shoulder
in this day and age	strong as an ox
it stands to reason	thin as a rail
kiss of death	truth is stranger than fiction
last but not least	white as a sheet

Rule No. 36:
Do not use clichés.

It is possible to use clichés in good writing. This is done by ***twisting the cliché***. "If necessity is the mother of invention, then laziness must be a first cousin." Some other examples: "to make a long story longer," "easier done than said." More examples of twisted clichés appear in Chapter 7.

Another place clichés may be used safely is in quotations. Everybody uses clichés in speaking, and sometimes they are worth capturing as direct quotations in order to convey the flavour of a person's comments.

In any event, if you are quoting someone who uses a cliché, then you should not alter the quote. Alterations of quotes are permitted to clean up grammar, but not the speaker's phrases.

Proverbs and Aphorisms

Like clichés, proverbs have been kicking around in the English language for a while, longer than clichés. Unlike clichés, however, they contain morals, and this extends their lifespan. It also makes them more palatable, if only marginally so.

A ***proverb*** is an old saying that expresses some commonsensical truth. Synonyms include *apothegm* and *adage*. Some people go so far as to call proverbs "the collective wisdom of mankind."

Usually a proverb is used metaphorically. "A stitch in time saves nine" is a proverb. Literally, it means, "If you sew a hole in your clothes before it gets big, you will have much less sewing to do." Metaphorically, it means, "Solve this problem now, and it will be easier to fix."

Some other examples of proverbs: "A bird in the hand is worth two in the bush" and "An apple a day keeps the doctor away."

English language proverbs in English language publications have the worn-out look of clichés. They should not be used. However, foreign proverbs translated into English are meaningful insights into another culture. "When you are on a mountain, you do not see its true shape" (Chinese). "A tree is known by its fruit" (Tagalog). "A nail that sticks up is hammered down" (both Japanese and Chinese).

For this reason, they are refreshing to read. They even can be the *angle* of a news story if the news event illustrates the proverb.[5] The ***angle*** of a story is the fact, or set of facts, that constitute the lead. Synonyms for *angle* are ***hook*** and ***peg***.

An ***aphorism*** is a short saying that expresses a common belief. Unlike a proverb, the aphorism is not used metaphorically:

> *Power tends to corrupt, and absolute power corrupts absolutely.*
> — Lord Acton

[5] For more on the *angle* of a news story, see Chapter 7.

Aphorisms are of questionable merit in the news; however, if a particular event is a strong illustration of an aphorism, then the aphorism itself may be alluded to without appearing trite.

Idioms

An ***idiom*** is a common phrase whose meaning is not obvious from its words. "He was *on all fours*" means "He was *on his hands and knees.*" "It was a *three-dog night*" means "It was a *very cold night.*"

English is highly idiomatic. The only way to learn idioms is to read and speak English a lot. The idiomatic patterns will become obvious with exposure.

Unlike proverbs and clichés, idioms can be used freely without harming the writing. Indeed, successful use of contemporary idiom makes writing sound stylish and sophisticated:

> "He'll be wearing a blue blazer," she said, then broke into a giggle. "And he's very tan." Gold pinkie ring, macho sport watch, tan infinitum.... Taki wiped some sweat in the Hay-Adams lobby. A five-block dash in the heat had temporarily impaired the power of his charm.

Here, *broke into a giggle* means *started to giggle impulsively and without warning*, and it is a very common idiom to convey this thought.

Another example of the highly idiomatic nature of English is the many uses of "shoot". Sometimes it is a noun, sometimes a verb, and sometimes an interjection. When used as an interjection, it usually is accompanied by an exclamation point: *"Shoot!" the lady muttered.* This means something like "Damn!", but "Shoot!" is more polite.

Here it is as a noun: "We went *on a turkey shoot.*" This means "We went *hunting for turkeys.*" People go on *photo shoots* when they go someplace to take photographs.

As a verb, "shoot" has many derived meanings: A person can *shoot a glance* at someone else, which means *glance quickly at. Shoot your mouth off* means to talk a lot and carelessly, and *shoot the works* means *invest everything. Shoot the wad* means *spend all the money.*

"Shoot" also has special meanings to drug addicts: To *shoot heroin* is to *inject heroin with a needle*, and a *shooting gallery* is a *place where addicts go to get drugs and "shoot up"*.

Finally, there is a difference between "shoot at" and "shoot in". To *shoot at* an object is to point a gun in the general direction of the object and pull the trigger; the phrase does not necessarily imply that a bullet hit the object. *Shoot in* implies that a bullet penetrated an object: "Wong was shot in the back" implies that a bullet struck Wong.

All of these uses of "shoot" are presented here to illistrate the idiomatic nature of English. There are many words like this with a multiplicity of meanings — "do", "get", and "take", are among them — but you can learn these special meanings only by immersing yourself in the language.

Jargon

Jargon is specialized vocabulary shared by a small group. Most professions have their own jargon, and this includes journalism (see Chapter 1 for examples).

Many writers lapse into jargon without realizing that the language is not understood by the audience. In the daily press, jargon creeps into court reports, as well as business and economic news. Legal terminology in news is known as ***legalese***, and it is the bane of court reporters.

Arbitrageur, hostile takeover, leveraged buyout.... Such terms surface in business reporting, and few people outside of the business world understand them.

Writers should use technical terms only sparingly, and, if they do use them, the writers should define the terms immediately.

Trendy Language

Journalists sometimes fall into the trap of using *fashionable language* consisting of coined words or old words used in new ways. Such language typically comes from bureaucratic settings — governments, military establishments, and big media, for example.

By "big media" I mean movie studios, mass circulation magazines, and television and radio networks. From big media come terms like *docudrama* (dramatization of a real event), *easy listening* (pleasing music), *Canto-pop* (Cantonese popular music), and *sitcom* (situation comedy). From the military come terms like *collateral damage* (civilian casualties caused by bombing), and *vertical insertion* (paratroop drop). From governments come terms like *flap potential* (potential for causing unpleasant public reaction), *through train* (continuity in Hong Kong's government through 1997, when mainland China assumes control), *fallback position* (originally a military term now used in reference to a secondary position that policymakers will take if the primary one becomes untenable), and *disinformation* (incorrect or misleading information deliberately leaked to the press).

Some contemporary media critics refer to this kind of language as ***newspeak***.[6] Writers should handle such language gingerly. It is an invaluable insight into the thinking of executives in the agencies that create the terms, but it can be easily overused, and many readers may not know the definitions.

By the way, *Time* is famous for its use of trendy language, so you should read that magazine if you want to learn this kind of language.

Slang

Slang is colourful, facetious or taboo language that is used only on certain occasions in selected groups. Terms from the drug culture are excellent examples: *ice, snow, weed, horse* and *acid* are, respectively, the slang terms for methamphetamine hydrochloride, cocaine, marijuana, heroine and lysergic acid di-ethylamide, or LSD.

Naturally, the journalist cannot use such language outside of direct quotations. Inside direct quotes, such language is an excellent means to capture the tone of a conversation, however.

Nevertheless, as Samuel Johnson once put it, "The pen must at length comply with the tongue." In other words, much slang loses its illegitimacy

---

[6] From Jonathan Green, *Newspeak: A Dictionary of Jargon* (Boston: Routledge and Kegan Paul, 1984).

and, in time, becomes acceptable language. Expressions like "get your act together" and "hassle", which were pure slang 20 years ago, are gaining respect, and they are used freely today by journalists.

Before leaving this section, it is important to note that the use of slang in the news changes the tone of the writing from formal to informal, a topic that is covered more thoroughly below, so the journalist should use it only when this is the objective.

Foreign Expressions

Foreign words and phrases are inappropriate in the news. This may seem to be a platitude, but many foreign expressions work their way into news reports anyway.

Three of the most common are *i.e., e.g.* and *etc.* All are Latin expressions, but beginning writers use them liberally in their work.

"I.e." is an abbreviation for *id est*, which translates literally as "that is". "E.g." means *exempli gratia*, or "for example". "Etc." means *et cetera*, or "and so forth".

There are common English expressions for all of these, and the English ones are preferred. The same goes for most other foreign expressions.

There are exceptions. At times, foreign words express new concepts for which English is ill-equipped. When it appears necessary to use a foreign word, it should be defined immediately if it is not in common use:

> He insisted that the *keiretsu*, Japan's groupings of industrial companies, had many positive features and that Japan was unlikely to bend to American demands that they be changed.

Many words like these come from diplomacy and international relations. *Detente, perestroika*, and *glasnost* are examples. All became common in English in recent years, so these may be used without definition.

The time when a foreign word becomes useable depends on its acceptance by the greater journalistic community. My own rule of thumb is this: *Use new foreign expressions without definition as soon as they begin appearing in mass circulation magazines and wire service reports.*

D.N.U.A.

Readers hate abbreviations. They are ugly. They are "noisy". They even are unnecessary. So why bother?

Look at this paragraph from one of my students who must have missed my lecture on this subject:

> Miss Tan started training at her uncle's dance company, the Malaysian Chinese Association Dance Group (M.C.A.). During her days in the A.P.A., she received training in American ballet.

A.P.A., M.C.A., U.S.A., A.A.A., M.B.A., A.M.A..... It looks like alphabet soup, and it doesn't take much of this to drive the reader batty — or at least to watching television news. In the last example, A.P.A. had been identified earlier in the piece as the Academy of Performing Arts. The writer could have written the paragraph this way instead:

> Miss Tan started training at her uncle's dance company, the Malaysian Chinese Association Dance Group. During her days in the academy, she received training in American ballet.

That's better. References to the Malaysian Chinese Association Dance Group could be as merely "the Malaysian troupe".

Rule No. 37:
Avoid abbreviations.

O.K., there are some exceptions: AIDS, U.S., VCR, IRA — any abbreviation you would use in everyday speech may be used in writing, but don't overdo it. After the first reference, AIDS could be called "the disease", U.S. could be called "America", and so on.

Rhetorical Questions

What is a rhetorical question?

Well, that last sentence is an example of one, and it's a truly insipid way to introduce a new topic.

A ***rhetorical question*** is *a question asked to produce an effect, not one asked to elicit a reply from the reader*. The effect that writers seek with rhetorical questions usually is to prepare the reader for a switch in topics. Beginning writers often use them as transitions, apparently because they cannot think of a better way to switch topics. Here's an example from one of my students:

> What are his views on education?
>
> Mr. Chun said a university education was not a necessary condition for financial success, although he believes that it may be an important means to experience personal growth.

This is a weak way to make the transition. An introductory phrase is sufficient, and it is more succinct:

> On the subject of education, Mr. Chun said a university education was not a necessary condition for financial success, although he believes that it may be an important means to experience personal growth.

Rule No. 38:
Do not rely on rhetorical questions for transitions.

There are many other ways to do the transition: "Regarding education", "Speaking about education", and so forth.

Sometimes rhetorical questions are designed to make an assertion, and in this use they are somewhat insipid also. Here's one from a travel writer with a weak imagination:

> SHANGHAI — Could anything be more exotic than a river journey down the Yangtze?

When I read this, I thought: *Yes, I suppose so. How about a weekend alone in an orbiting space station with Madonna and a case of V.O cognac?* I'm only kidding, of course. But, as you can see, the rhetorical question is an invitation to the reader to *counterargue* with you — that is, to get into a debate with you about your views. If you lose the debate, then you are likely to lose the reader as well. When you lose your audience, you have failed as a writer.

Parallel Structures

Parallel structures are repeated patterns in writing. They exist at every level. There can be parallel phrases in sentences. There can be parallel sentences in paragraphs. There can be parallel paragraphs in chapters. There can be parallel chapters in books.

Those last four sentences are parallel. Here is a sentence that is not parallel:

> During her days at the academy, Miss Tan received training in American ballet and choreography and had lectures on art history.

Now, here is a revision that makes that sentence parallel:

> During her days at the academy, Miss Tan studied American ballet, choreography and art history.

Parallel structures are strong, and they lubricate the communication. They prepare the reader for what follows.

For additional examples of parallel structures, see the profile *taki* in Chapter 8.

Punctuation

Exclamation points indicate excitement, surprise, incredulity, a high degree of emotion. Here is a paragraph from a student who wrote a profile of a ballet dancer:

> Miss Tan was at last granted special permission after persistent requests for a screening examination. In the examination for the ballet stream, she presented a piece of Chinese folk dance!

Whoa! Who is surprised here? The writer? If so, the writer is losing her objectivity.

> **Rule No. 39:**
> ***Do not use exclamation points outside direct quotes.***

Exclamation points may be used as part of direct quotes when someone is yelling, however:

"On the floor!" shouted the masked man to customers.

They may also be used to express strong emotion, but only in quotations:

"How beautiful! Amazing!"

Another way to create emphasis is by using capital letters, but you should not do this. This is a technique favoured by beginning writers. They use capital letters like this: *"That's AMAZING!"*

When all the letters in a word are capitalized, we say it is ***all caps***.

Here is a rule about all caps:

Rule No. 40:
Do not write body copy in all caps.

By ***body copy***, I mean the text of a news story. Rather than using all capitals for emphasis, it is better to find some other way to make the point.

One final rule: Avoid parentheses. Many editors dislike them. Parentheses are generally overworked, and the journalist should find alternative ways of expressing parenthetical matter.

Especially objectionable is the style of many beginning writers to put an abbreviation in parentheses after a full proper name — *The Association of Southeast Asian Nations (ASEAN)....* The abbreviation itself is objectionable, so its use should not be multiplied unnecessarily.

The professional writer can introduce the abbreviation without the parentheses merely by placing it in a nearby subsequent sentence and allowing the reader to draw the inference — *The Association of Southeast Asian Nations agreed Monday to a regional security pact in the region. ASEAN, whose members have opposed such a pact in the past....*

There are times when parentheses are useful, however, and their application at these times is not disputed. One application is to insert clarification, and often this is done inside a direct quotation — *The Prime Minister said England would spend "about £2 million (HK$28 million)" on Hong Kong's defense prior to 1997*. Another example — *The Governor said he was "looking forward to meeting (Chinese Foreign Minister) Mr. Li Peng" on his first trip to Beijing*. The second example assumes that Mr. Li's title had not been provided previously in the story.

If a story is well crafted, then such applications will be unnecessary. In the last example, it would have been a simple matter to introduce the foreign minister's name and title in a paragraph preceding the quote.

If you love to use *brackets*, [ ], and *braces*, { }, then you should be a mathematician. These are not used in the news.

Sexist Language

Sexist language is language that expresses gender — policeman, fireman, stewardess, maid. There are genderless alternatives to each of these — police officer, firefighter, flight attendant, domestic helper.

Rule No. 41:
Avoid sexist language.

The problem with sexist language is that it promotes stereotypes. Modern societies have seen traditional male roles assumed by women, so the language is dated. It has become a political issue.

Table 2.2 Sexist language and genderless alternatives

chairman	chair, presiding officer
fathers	ancestors, parents, forebears
fireman	firefighter
forefathers	forebears, pioneers
housewife	homemaker
mailman	mail carrier
man	person, individual, one
mankind	humanity, human race
men	people, human beings
policeman	police officer
spokesman	representative
statesman	leader, diplomat
watchman	security guard, guard
workman	worker

One attempt to avoid sexist language was the creation of the title *Ms.* Its use is discussed more fully on Page 48. This title was introduced as a means to avoid sexist connotations of Mrs.

Meanwhile, many contemporary newspaper editors are asking writers to seek alternatives to common sexist words.

Provincialisms

Journalists must be cautious also in their use of provincialisms. ***Provincialisms*** are words that are peculiar to a specific region. Sometimes they are called *regionalisms.*

If the audience is strictly the local audience, then provincialisms may be acceptable. In Southeast Asia, for example, *godown, hong* and *taipan* are provincialisms. In Singapore a journalist can safely write about a fire at some taipan's godown without confusing the audience, because most people there know that a taipan is a chief business executive and a godown is a warehouse. If the story were being transmitted overseas, however, alternative language would be necessary, because American and British audiences would not recognize the terms.

It is difficult to identify provincialisms. People are immersed in their own cultures. Like fish in water, they do not see their own language, so they are unaware of peculiarities in local usage. For this reason, it is wise for journalists to cultivate an interest in how English is used outside their own communities.

Tone

In writing, the word ***tone*** refers to the degree of formality. The range is from *formal* to *informal.*

The most formal writing in English is found in legal documents. Legal writing should be precise, and it tends to employ the language of the courts, which is somewhat antiquated. There is no place for slang or contemporary idiom in legal documents. Nor is there a place for such literary devices as humour, sarcasm or irony.

Here is an example of legal writing:

> A seditious intention is an intention
>
> (a) to bring into hatred or contempt or to excite disaffection against the person of Her Majesty, or Her Heirs or Successors, or against the Government of Hong Kong, or the government of any other part of Her Majesty's dominions or of any territory under Her Majesty's protection as by law established;
>
> (b) to excite Her Majesty's subjects or inhabitants of Hong Kong to attempt to procure the alteration, otherwise than by lawful means, of any other matter in Hong Kong as by law established; or
>
> (c) to bring into hatred or contempt or to excite disaffection against the administration of justice in Hong Kong; or
>
> (d) to raise discontent or disaffection amongst Her Majesty's subjects or inhabitants of Hong Kong; or
>
> (e) to promote feelings of ill-will and enmity between different classes of the population of Hong Kong; or
>
> (f) to incite persons to violence; or
>
> (g) to counsel disobedience to law or to any lawful order.[7]

This is a fairly typical example of legal writing, which is probably the most formal style that can be found in English. It is distinguished by long sentences with complex punctuation, big words, and antiquated syntax.

Even though it is broken into several paragraphs, this is actually one sentence. The sentence has 174 words and six semicolons. Phrases like *excite disaffection* and *promote enmity* are stuffy, old fashioned ways to say *make people disloyal* and *make people hate each other*. And *as by law established* contains an inverted word order: Normally, one would write *as established by law*. In former days, English, like contemporary German, had more word endings, and these governed the roles of words in sentences, so word order was less important than it is today. As a consequence, people who are trying to sound formal and old fashioned in their writing often invert the order of words. The result is rather silly.

[7] *Laws of Hong Kong*, Vol. 14, Chapter 200, Part II, Section 9.

Courtesy Titles

Words like *Mr., Mrs.*, and *Miss* are called ***courtesy titles***. In the U.K., they may be called ***honorific titles***. Journalists use them as a courtesy. American journalists have eliminated them in almost all contexts, so even the president of the United States, after the first reference, is referred to routinely by his last name only: *In Cleveland Monday for a Democratic fund-raiser, Clinton told crowds....* However, they are still in wide use in the U.K.

Married women who prefer to use their maiden names are referred to as "Miss", so it's *Miss Elizabeth Taylor* even though she has been married quadzillion times.

Ms came into use in the 1950s, but a few newspaper editors refuse to use it. It was promoted by the women's movement as an women's equivalent to "Mr.", which does not reveal a man's marital status. Editors generally will use whatever courtesy title a woman uses herself, so it is the duty of the journalist to ask women about their preferences in this regard.

When referring to a couple, it is customary to refer to them as "Mr. and Mrs.", as in *Mr. and Mrs. Kenneth Leung*. Some women prefer to be known only by their husbands' name, and the journalist should respect their preferences in this regard: *Mrs. Robert Bond....*

Honorific titles also include *Lord, Dr.*, and *Sir*. In all cases, courtesy titles are not followed by a full stop in British usage, but they are in American usage.

Because there is no rigid standard on this subject, you should consult your editors about their preferences regarding courtesy titles and adhere to their recommendations.

3

The Inverted Pyramid

There are several common ways to write news, but the most common one — and certainly the easiest — is the inverted pyramid. Because it is so easy to use, it is the first one introduced here.

The ***inverted pyramid*** gets its name from the order in which the facts are presented in the news story. The facts are presented in descending order of importance. More important facts are high in the story. Less important ones are at the bottom.

The inverted pyramid is used every day at daily newspapers. It is not common in magazines.

The value of the inverted pyramid in reporting news is due in part to production requirements. In ***copy fitting*** — that is, in arranging news stories on the pages of a newspaper — editors and compositors often ***cut*** stories in order to make them fit in the available space. *If the least important facts are at the bottom of a story, then editors can cut from the bottom up without losing the most important information.* This expedites the production process: If an editor wants to shorten a story, he or she doesn't have to search through the entire story looking for unimportant information to cut out. It's all at the bottom.

Aware of this practice, the veteran journalist will avoid placing important details at the end of a piece. On those occasions when it is inappropriate to cut a piece, the journalist will inform the editors. *Do not cut* is a common phrase used to convey this concern.

The inverted pyramid can be broken down into component parts. The first paragraph is called the lead and the second paragraph is called the supporting paragraph. The rest of the story may be classified as either secondary information or as background material.

The components of the inverted pyramid will be discussed in the order in which they appear in a typical news story. Let's start with the lead.

The Lead

The ***lead*** is one-paragraph summary of the news event that is being reported. Because it summarizes the event, this kind of lead is sometimes called a ***summary lead***.

There are a few rules of thumb about summary leads for inverted pyramids. One very basic rule of thumb is:

Rule No. 11:
Write summary leads in one short sentence.

Here are a few examples:

SAN SEBASTIAN, Spain — Spain expects 32 million tourists this year, 13 percent more than last year.

MOSCOW — The first spacewoman got her first pair of false eyelashes Monday.

ATHENS, Greece — A riot erupted Monday in Averoff Prison over the death of a political detainee ill with tuberculosis.

Note that each of these leads is a single paragraph.

Rule No. 12:
Write summary leads as a single paragraph.

Also note the lengths of these leads. They are 13, 11, and 17 words long, respectively. These look easy to write, but this is only because they were written by professionals. In fact, it is not easy to write good leads that are this short — usually because situtations are too complicated to summarize in so few words.

In fact, longer leads are tolerable, but I have limits:

Rule No. 13:
Strive for leads of 20 to 25 words.

Summary leads of 15 words or less are on the short side. Leads of 35 words or more are definitely too long.

In glancing through a newspaper, you will see many leads that do not conform to these rules. Many of them are ***featurized leads***, and these will be taken up in Chapter 7.

In crafting a summary lead, the journalist considers these questions: Who was involved? What was the event? Where did the event occur? When did the event occur? And why did the event occur? Journalists call these ***the Five W's:*** *Who, What, When, Where* and *Why.*

Following is a typical example:

> BANGKOK — A maintenance worker plunged 20 storeys down an elevator shaft Tuesday and suffered only a fractured ankle and hand cuts.

Who? A maintenance worker. What? A fall down an elevator shaft. When? Tuesday. Where? Bangkok.

Why this happened is not established in the lead. This is because the causes of events are sometimes complex, and their explanations take too many words. As a result, the causes are sometimes delayed to a subsequent paragraph.

Here is another example:

> STOCKHOLM — A concert by American soul singer Ray Charles was cancelled Monday because he is on a United Nations blacklist for performing in South Africa.

One difference between these two examples is that the "why" is given in the second lead. This is because the "why" is the most important part of the story. Another interesting difference is that the "who" in the first lead is not identified by name, while the "who" in the second lead *is* identified by name. This is also because the "who" in the second story is a very important part of the story. Most readers would not recognize the name of the subject of the first story; on the other hand, the subject of the second story is well-known. Indeed, it's his stature as a recording artist that makes the Stockholm event newsworthy.

Imagine how weak the second lead would have seemed if it had been written like this:

> STOCKHOLM — A concert by an American soul singer was cancelled Monday because he is on a United Nations blacklist for performing in South Africa.

The first example above is known as a delayed lead. A synonym is blind lead. A ***delayed*** or ***blind lead*** is a kind of summary lead that delays specific details of names or places to subsequent paragraphs. Conversely, an ***immediate identification lead*** is a kind of summary lead that specifically identifies people or places. The second example above is an immediate identification lead.

A rule of thumb about which of these to use is this:

Rule No. 14:
Use an immediate I.D. lead only if the news event concerns a famous person, place or thing.

Here is another example of a blind lead:

> NEW YORK — A 32-year-old stockbroker who just learned that he had AIDS plunged to his death Monday after leaping from the observation deck of the Empire State Building.

People jump to their deaths every day without making the news. But a jump from one of the tallest buildings in the world is visually powerful — so the building is specifically identified in the lead.

In short, a summary lead is a one-sentence summary of a news event, and it may be either blind or immediate I.D., depending on how well-known the people, places and things are.

Second-Day Leads

This kind of lead is used to freshen up a story that is a day or two old. Here's a formal definition: A ***second-day lead*** is *a lead that updates an old news event by providing the reader with the most recent development.*

Example:

> HONG KONG — Two dozen Chinese porkers wandered aimlessly around Tai Wai early Monday after a freight car derailed in Sha Tin.
>
> The accident occurred late Sunday, when a faulty yard switch sent the Chinese railway car down a siding with 40 pigs aboard, ramming it into a bumper and throwing open the door.

The ***hook***, ***angle***, or ***peg*** of this story is the obvious humour evoked by the sight of pigs wandering around an urban setting. In searching for a *fresh angle*, therefore, an editor might ask a reporter, "What's your angle?" or "What are you going peg this on?" or "What are you going to hang this story on?", because pegs are often used to hang things. For more on this, see Chapter 7.

As is obvious from this example, the second-day lead is useful if the journalist *missed the story*, or didn't get the details at the time it happened, as is often the case for events occurring late at night or in the wee hours of the morning.

This kind of lead is also useful for putting a different *spin*, or approach, on a story that has been widely reported in electronic media. This technique is commonly used in reporting about major sporting events, which are broadcast live on television, so the print journalist must be creative in writing the lead.

> ISTANBUL — "Where East Meets West" has long been the moniker for this busy port on the Bosporus. This was literally true Monday as Manchester United, the English champions, took on Galatasaray at Ali Sami Yen stadium in the first round of European football's UEFA Cup match.
>
> Seven hundred Manchester supporters witnessed United winger Lee Sharpe score a last-minute penalty kick that put United into the second round of the competition.

Technically speaking, this is not a summary lead, but a ***featurized lead***. This kind of lead is discussed fully in Chapter 7.

In a story such as this, thousands of football fans in the audience already know the results of the game from having viewed it on television. This puts the print journalist in the difficult position of making day-old news readable and interesting, and the second-day lead is a clever way to do this.

Common Problems in Lead Writing

There are a few pitfalls in lead writing. Seven of them will be discussed here: subordination of material in the lead; leading with a series; leading with a direct quotation; leading with a question; backing into the lead; burying the lead; and writing a say-nothing lead.

First, I will show you an example of subordination of material in the lead:

> PARIS — President Jacques Chirac, under fire for French nuclear tests in the South Pacific, said Wednesday his nation would complete the nuclear test programme in February next year rather than May, as originally planned.

The subordinated material in question here is "under fire for French nuclear tests in the South Pacific". This phrase requires the reader to slow down and process this lesser important information before he can go to the main idea.

In English grammar, **subordination** is *the placement of relatively unimportant text within a main idea for the purpose of modifying it.* There is nothing wrong with subordinating material subsequently in the story. But one of the virtues of good leads is that they take the reader quickly and efficiently into the story.

Rule No. 15:
Do not subordinate material in the lead.

The above lead could have been written without the subordinated material, like this:

> PARIS — President Jacques Chirac Wednesday said France would cut back on its nuclear test programme in the South Pacific.
>
> In the face of stiff international criticism, Mr. Chirac said the programme would end in February rather than May, as originally planned.

Do you sense how much easier it is "to get into the story" in the second version of the lead? In the second version, the subordinated material has been moved down into the supporting graf. The subordinated material is more appropriate there because the international opposition to the French nuclear test programme was old news, so it served more as background information than new information.

By the way, whether you write "said Wednesday", as in the first version of the lead, or "Wednesday said", as in the second version, is largely a matter of the rhythm. Both forms are correct.

Turning now to **leading with a series**, I will illustrate the problem with an example:

> A population explosion, a decrease in natural resources, the deterioration of the environment, and damage to the ecology are critical problems facing the modernization of China, one of the nation's leading physicists said Thursday.

This lead was written by one of my students who covered a speech by Dr. Zhou Guangzhao, director of the Chinese Academy of Sciences. The subject of the sentence is a wordy, four-element series, and it takes the reader a long time to get to the main point. Part of the problem is that *each comma acts as a soft stop that blocks the reader's processing of the information.* The focus of Dr. Zhou's speech was China's modernization programme. If possible, this should be the subject of the sentence.

The lead also is redundant — *the deterioration of the environment, and damage to the ecology* express closely related ideas — and it misuses the word "ecology". Like most words ending in "-ology", ecology is a science. *Ecology is the study of organisms in relation to their environments*, and the word is often mistakenly used in place of "environment".

Look how much better the lead is when flipped around. Now the subject of the sentence is also the subject of the story, and the bulky series is in the predicate of the sentence:

> China's modernization programme is handicapped by population growth, environmental deterioration, and depletion of natural resources, a leading Chinese physicist said Thursday.

Here's another rule of thumb:

> **Rule No. 16:**
> ***Do not lead with a series.***

As usual, you will see exceptions. There will be times when a series can be a refreshing alternative to the summary lead:

> WASHINGTON — Neither jogging, nor Lean Cuisine, nor health spas, nor Jane Fonda, nor "lite" beer, nor two decades of nagging from U.S. health agencies appears to have done much to reduce the national prevalence of fat.
>
> Americans are just as likely to be overweight today as they were in the 1960s, according to a report from the U.S. Centers for Disease Control.[1]

This story easily could have been handled routinely with a summary lead, but the story has a humorous side to it, so the writer chose to ***soften*** the lead, to ***featurize*** it.

Now for some comments on ***leading with a direct quotation***. Here's an example:

> "Hong Kong has an imperative moral responsibility to promote the cause of the modernization of China," a prominent Chinese physicist said Thursday.

This lead came from another student covering the Zhou speech mentioned above. There are two basic problems with direct quotations as leads: One is that leads should be summaries, and a direct quotation doesn't have the ring of a summary — it doesn't look or sound like one. The other is that direct quotations almost always can be brushed up, improved upon.

Rule No. 17:
Do not lead with a direct quotation.

The last lead could be written like this:

> Hong Kong has a duty to help China modernize, a prominent Chinese physicist said Thursday.

When a lead is this short, there is room to add something. In this case, "imperative moral responsibility" is rather strong language. Journalists often use partial quotes in leads to capture the mood or tone of a speaker's remarks. Here is the way to do it:

---

[1] *International Herald Tribune*, Hong Kong, Monday, 15 July 1991, No. 33,750, p. 1.

> Hong Kong has an "imperative moral responsibility" to help China modernize, a prominent Chinese physicist said Thursday.

Once in a rare while, journalists find that a direct quotation lends itself well to the lead. For an example, see Chapter 7.

Leading with a question also is weak. There are two principal problems with questions as leads: One is that journalists are in the business of answering questions for their readers, not asking them; and the other is that, if the reader does not relate to the question, it will turn the reader away:

> DUBAI, United Arab Emirates — Have you ever wondered what it would feel like to be selected as Miss UAE for 1995?

When I read this, I thought: *No, I haven't, thank you.* This is a strange question to put to men, and they are at least 50 percent of the newspaper audience. In posing an irrelevant question, the journalist loses readers.

Rule No. 18:
Do not lead with a question.

There are exceptions to this rule. There are times, for example, when a question is the focus of a news story:

> CAMBRIDGE, Mass. — How many dimples are on a golf ball? Ans.: 336.
>
> This was the deciding question Monday as America's whiz kids gathered to compete in the 11th annual Trivia Quiz Contest at Massachusetts Institute of Technology.

In this case a question was an integral part of the news. In any event, the question should not be used as a rhetorical device attempting to grab the reader's attention. For more on rhetorical questions, see Chapter 2.

Backing into the lead is *beginning a lead with a long introductory phrase*:

> HONG KONG — Asserting that air services are "running absolutely normally and passengers should turn up for flights as usual," a Cathay Pacific spokesman Monday said the airline is due for another round of talks with flight attendants who have threatened a walkout.

Rule No. 19:
Do not back into the lead.

The 17-word introductory phrase in the last lead delays the main point of the story. Short introductory phrases are acceptable, but even short ones should be used sparingly in leads:

> HOLLYWOOD — At an age when most major actors are grateful for a walk-on, 67-year-old Lauren Bacall is getting strong supporting roles. Hollywood hasn't had enough of "The Look", as she is known.[2]

Even this 12-word introductory phrase is long-ish, from my point of view, but it's better than the previous one.

The next problem is burying the lead. ***Burying the lead*** is placing the most important point deep in the story.

> HONG KONG — In an unprecedented move, Police Commissioner Li Kwan-ha met with legislators Monday to discuss enforcement procedures against smugglers.
>
> It was the first time that a commissioner of police has addressed the Legislative Council.
>
> The commissioner said armed, uniformed Chinese mainland border guards threatened officers of the Marine Police who attempted to board a vessel suspected of smuggling Sunday night.

This is a story with the makings of a major international incident, but the reader would never know it from the lead. The third paragraph would make a better lead:

> HONG KONG — The commissioner of police Monday said armed, uniformed Chinese mainland border guards recently threatened officers of the Marine Police who attempted to board a vessel suspected of smuggling.

---

[2] *South China Morning Post*, Hong Kong, Friday, 27 December 1991, Vol. 47, No. 358, p. 16.

Rule No. 20:
Do not bury the lead.

Finally, there is the so-called ***say-nothing lead***. This is a lead that doesn't contain the essential information that the reader expects to find in the first paragraph.

Here is an example:

> TAIPEI — The president of the Taiwan Medical Association gave a speech Monday at the opening ceremonies of a new hospital in central Taipei.

If you are like most readers, you are not interested in the fact that someone *gives a speech*. You are interested in *what is said* during the speech. In short, *the lead should not be that someone gave a speech, but a summary of the main idea*:

> TAIPEI — The president of the Taiwan Medical Association Monday called for national health insurance during a hospital dedication in central Taipei.

Rule No. 21:
Do not write say-nothing leads.

Because this problem of say-nothing leads occurs so often in reporting speeches, it is discussed again in Chapter 5.

Now that we have covered leads in some detail, let's turn our attention to the second paragraph of the inverted pyramid, often called the supporting paragraph.

The Supporting Paragraph

Leads are so sketchy that the journalist needs to establish more detail right away. This is the job of the second paragraph, which is known as the supporting paragraph.

The ***supporting paragraph*** is a paragraph following the lead that expands or amplifies the lead.

> BANGKOK — A maintenance worker plunged 20 storeys down an elevator shaft Tuesday and suffered only a fractured ankle and hand cuts.
>
> Mr. Willie Samsap, 26, was servicing lift cables in the top floor of the Bank of Islam building when he lost his balance and tumbled into the shaft.

In this supporting paragraph, the journalist has specifically identified the subject and provided the "why".

Rule No. 22:
Make the supporting paragraph parallel to the lead.

You learned in Chapter 2 that parallel structures strengthen your writing. The last lead is an example of a parallel structure. In the above example, the lead and supporting paragraph are constructed in similar fashion. That is, the subject of the lead is the subject of the supporting paragraph. It is easy for the reader to *get into* the story, as some journalists would say.

Here is another example:

> MOSCOW — The first spacewoman got her first false eyelashes Monday.
>
> Valentina Tereshkova got the eyelashes as a gift from the American Women for International Understanding.

Secondary Information

If the lead presents the most important information about an event, then the remaining information must be relegated to lower status. It thus gets a lower position in the story.

For the sake of discussion, information that is not in the lead or in the supporting paragraph is ***secondary information***. This is the sum total of all the miscellany and detail that strikes the journalist as relevant but not worth putting in the lead.

There is a special kind of secondary information, and usually this information has been published in previous editions of the newspaper. This information is ***background information***, and it is information inserted in the story wherever appropriate to bring the reader up to date, to remind him about the context of current developments.

An example of background information is provided in the news story about a jewellery store robbery below. The last paragraph in this story is background information.

Story Organization

There are two main ways to organize a story written in inverted pyramid style — chronological and nonchronological. After the lead and supporting paragraph, the ***chronological story*** is one that describes developments of a news event in the same order that they occurred in time. In this sense, they are like the narrative form, which is discussed in more detail in Chapter 9.

The chronology is widely used for major crimes and disasters, events that require blow-by-blow accounts. Following is a compiled story about a robbery in Hong Kong that I pulled together from various news accounts. It is written in chronological order:

$2.5 million stolen in daring noontime robbery

1 HONG KONG — Armed robbers escaped with $2.5 million in gold and precious stones Monday afternoon in a daring lunchtime holdup of a Tsim Sha Tsui jewellery in Kowloon.

2 Police said they have no suspects in the case, which resulted in a police chase through Hung Hom and the Walled City.

3 It was the 10th armed robbery of a jewellery store this year, and the third of the Christmas season.

4 Witnesses said that three men, two with handguns and one with a knife, entered Wong Yee Jewellery about 12:25 p.m.

5 Two customers and three staff members were in the store at the time, and the robbers demanded that everyone lie on the floor.

6 All of the men wore dark clothing, gloves and training shoes, and they spoke to one another in Mandarin rather than Cantonese, according to one witness.

7 One of them used the butt of his pistol to smash three display cases containing precious stones and gold items. These were scooped up and put into a cloth bag carried by one of the men.

8 Meanwhile, Mr. Wong Iam Ching, the proprietor of the store, pressed a silent alarm that alerted police.

9 The men leapt into a waiting white Toyota driven by a fourth man, and they sped away toward Kai Tak Airport. As the robbers pulled away from the kerb, two police vehicles converged on the scene and chased the robbers' car through Hung Hom.

10 The robbers' car sideswiped a Kowloon Motor Bus, went out of control, and crashed into a flyway abutment near the Walled City.

11 The robbers ran from the car into a pedestrian subway, where they escaped.

12 Police said the robbery bears similarity to one held two weeks ago on Hong Kong Island, when $1.1 million in jewellery was stolen.

Telling this story chronologically makes it easy to understand. In this story, ***Paragraph 1*** is a summary lead, ***Paragraph 2*** is a supporting paragraph, ***Paragraph 3*** is background information, ***Paragraphs 4–11*** are secondary information presented in order of occurrence, and ***Paragraph 12*** is background information that may be cut if the story is too long.

Some chronological stories give specific times for the events being reported. Notice that in the following piece, which ran as a sidebar to a major air disaster, the material that follows the times is written in *present tense*:

Pilot ignored warning on emergency landing

1 The pilot of the ill-fated Israeli cargo jet fought with air controllers over the approach for an emergency landing, Dutch officials conceded Monday night.

2 Mr. Theo Croon, director of tower approach at Schiphol airport, said the controllers assigned the pilot Schiphol's runway No. 6 as the "most logical solution because it would have taken the plane away from an inhabited zone."

3 But Captain Isaach Fuchs insisted on using No. 27, ignoring warnings that he would have a tail wind, making braking more difficult.

4 Mr. Croon was at a loss to justify the pilot's insistence on Runway 27. Under emergency protocol the pilot has the final say.

5 Officials gave the following version of the flight's final moments — 15 minutes from take-off to the crash:

6 6:21 p.m.: Plane takes off to north, climbing slowly because of strong wind and the plane's weight. Jet tracks a broad arc to the east according to standard procedures.

7 6:27 p.m.: About 28 kilometres east of airport, pilot radios "May Day". He says fire has broken out in the No. 3 engine and requests permission for emergency landing. Plane appeared still to be under control. With plane at 1,525 metres, pilot reports fire in No. 4 engine and loss of flaps and control over the craft.

8 6:33 p.m.: "Going down," says frantic pilot.

9 6:36 p.m.: Jumbo slams into apartment nine minutes after "May Day" alert.

Sometimes I refer to a story with specific times in it as a ***hard chronology***. The chronological story about the robbery I call a ***soft chronology*** because the exact times of events are unknown; only the order of the events is known.

Rule No. 31:
Use present tense after specific times when writing a hard chronology.

Turning now to the ***nonchronological story***, this is one which places events more or less in descending order of importance. In the following example of a nonchronological story, the time sequence of the various developments is treated as though it were irrelevant:

40,000 dial in to listen to recording[3]

1 More than 40,000 people telephoned *The Sun* newspaper Tuesday to listen to a recording of an alleged telephone conversation between the Princess of Wales and a man called James.

2 Listening to the entire saga would have put £11 (HK$169) on their telephone bills, and the newspaper said it would give the expected £50,000 profit to the National Society for the Prevention of Cruelty to children.

3 Mr. Cyril Reenan, a retired bank manager living in Abingdon, Oxfordshire, was the radio amateur with the scanning device and the large aerial in his tree who on New Year's Eve 1989 stumbled across the conversation. It was said to have taken place between the princess at Sandringham and an amorous caller using a mobile telephone.

4 Mr. Reenan claimed that he and his wife had picked up the conversation by accident while amusing themselves with the electronic gadget.

5 The postal worker who regularly delivers to their two-storey brick home condemned the former bank manager as a "nosey old bugger".

6 "I'm very surprised by his behaviour. I'm just glad he was not my bank manager," mail carrier Gerald Rouse said.

7 The Sun newspaper dubbed Mr. Reenan's "Secret Squirrel", after an animated cartoon character who used bizarre-looking listening devices to track down criminals.

8 Listening to other people's telephone conversations is an offence under the Wireless Telegraphy Act, 1949, and the Interception of Communications Act, 1985, punishable by up to two years in jail and a fine of up to £2,000.

[3] *South China Morning Post*, vol. 48, no. 238, Thursday, 27 August 1992, p. 13.

9 But Scotland Yard reaffirmed that it had no plans to investigate the offence. Buckingham Palace, although saying nothing officially on the matter, indicated that it had not asked police to become involved.

10 The Press Complaints Commission has reported a surprisingly low level of public disapproval at recent intrusions into royal privacy.

This story is built piecemeal with facts from 1989, as well as as "Tuesday" and probably several other unidentified times. But they are not presented in the order in which they occurred — hence the expression "nonchronological".

The eighth paragraph, by the way, is another example of background information.

4

The Multiple-Element Story

The ***multiple-element story*** is an inverted pyramid that deals with two or more related news events simultaneously.

The story takes several forms, but they are easy to learn. Once grasped, the different forms of the multiple-element story are powerful alternatives to the inverted pyramid, especially for journalists who are writing about complex situations.

The most obvious application is in news coverage of legislative bodies — parliaments, councils and congresses, for example. The reason is that a legislative body rarely takes only a single action in one meeting. The typical meeting of a legislative body will touch upon several issues.

Another obvious application lies in international diplomacy. A major diplomatic initiative in Paris may result in a response from Algeria. These could be written as separate news events, but they are easily and efficiently handled with the multiple-element story.

Another obvious application is in compiling stories from the wire services. ***Compiling*** is *combining two or more stories into one*. The wire services often send separate but related stories that may be combined as a multiple-element story.

Multiple-Element Leads

As in the inverted pyramid, the first paragraph of a multiple-element story is the lead. It is a summary lead in the conventional sense. It differs only in that it deals with two events.

To illustrate the multiple-element lead, let's start with two separate leads from different parts of the world that are somehow related, but are based on entirely different news events. First, here is a lead from Burma:

> RANGOON, Burma — Troops invaded a university campus Tuesday as hundreds of flag-waving students demanded the release of jailed opposition leader Aung San Suu Kyi.

Now, here is a related lead from Norway:

> OSLO, Norway — The eldest son of jailed Burmese leader Aung San Suu Kyi Tuesday accepted a Nobel Peace Prize on her behalf, saying he accepted it "in the name of all the people of Burma."

An experienced editor could easily combine these into a multiple-element lead, like this:

> Hundreds of university students in Rangoon protested against the military junta in Burma Tuesday as the eldest son of jailed opposition leader Aung San Suu Kyi accepted a Nobel Peace Prize on her behalf in Oslo, Norway.

As is the custom when writing news originating in two locations, there is no dateline on this story.

The main problem with a multiple-element lead is space. It is difficult to summarize two events in one 35-word sentence. This is especially true if the events are complex.

If it is difficult to summarize events in one sentence, journalists break the rule about single paragraph leads. They write a lead in two paragraphs, like this:

> Troops invaded a Rangoon university campus Tuesday as hundreds of flag-waving students demanded the release of jailed Burmese opposition leader Aung San Suu Kyi.
>
> In Oslo, Aung San Suu Kyi's eldest son accepted a Nobel Peace Prize on her behalf, saying he accepted the award "in the name of all the people of Burma."

In this example, the two-word phrase "In Oslo" acts as a transition between reports of the two events. Short, simple transitions like this one play an important role in writing the multiple-element story.

Supporting Paragraphs

As in the inverted pyramid, the properly built multiple-element story will have supporting paragraphs. Two events call for two supporting paragraphs. One supporting paragraph is placed immediately after the multiple-element lead, like this:

> Hundreds of Rangoon university students protested the military junta in Burma Tuesday as the eldest son of jailed opposition leader Aung San Suu Kyi accepted a Nobel Peace Prize on her behalf in Oslo, Norway.
>
> In Rangoon, a crowd of 2,000 gathered on University Avenue while riot police and soldiers with machine guns surrounded the campus to break up the mid-morning student rally.

The lead jumps from Rangoon to Oslo, so the transition "In Rangoon" opened the second paragraph to bring the reader back to Burma.

Rule No. 32:
Provide obvious transitions when shifting focus over time or distance.

Now that the lead and one supporting paragraph have been established for the Rangoon part of the story, it is a straighforward matter to polish off the Burmese events with the standard inverted pyramid.

Then, once the Burmese story has been fully developed, a transition to Oslo introduces the supporting paragraph for the Norwegian segment. Then the entire Norwegian event is told. This concludes the story.

Here is how the entire story would look if crafted in this fashion:

> Hundreds of university students in Rangoon protested military rule in Burma Tuesday as relatives of jailed opposition leader Aung San Suu Kyi accepted a Nobel Peace Prize on her behalf in Oslo, Norway.
>
> In Rangoon, a crowd of 2,000 gathered on University Avenue as riot police and soldiers with machine guns marshalled outside the campus in preparation to break up the mid-morning student rally.

It was the first significant pro-democracy demonstration since mid-1989.

Inside Rangoon University, hundreds of flag-waving students marched near the university's convocation hall, shouting demands for the release of Aung San Suu Kyi, who has been under house arrest since July 1989.

Under the personal supervision of General Myo Nyunt, the military commander in Rangoon, troops sealed off University Avenue to traffic and encircled the campus.

General Nyunt is a senior member of the ruling State Law and Order Restoration Council, the official name of the military junta that rules Burma.

In Oslo, Aung San Suu Kyi's eldest son Mr. Alexander Aris, 18, said he was accepting the prize "in the name of all the people of Burma".

"My mother would say this prize belongs not to her but to all those men, women and children, who, even as I speak, continue to sacrifice their well-being, their freedom and their lives in pursuit of a democratic Burma," he said.

Aung San Suu Kyi, 46, could not accept the US$1 million (HK$7.76 million) prize in person because Burma's military junta has said it will not allow her to return if she leaves the country.

She has been under house arrest since July 1989.

Mr. Aris was joined at the award ceremony in Oslo City Hall by his 14-year-old brother, Kim, and their father, Mr. Michael Aris, a British academic.

More than 1,500 people, including Norway's King Harald V and Queen Sonja, government members, Burmese exiles and former laureates, attended the ceremony.

One of the most important features of multiple-element stories — and a feature that is often overlooked by beginning writers — is the transition. Naturally, if a journalist is writing about events in two different places, he must make it clear to the reader which place he is writing about at any given time. The transition does this.

In the above story, transitions occur in Paragraphs 2 and 7. A list of obvious transitional phrases appears in Table 4.1.

Table 4.1 Transitional Phrases

Alternatively	On the other hand
Elsewhere	In Tokyo
Later	Today in Hanoi
Yesterday	However
Just last week	Although
Because	Since
Moreover	Nevertheless
Similarly	Consequently
Subsequently	First, second, *etc.*
As a result	Instead
Finally	In spite of

Transitions in Compiled Stories

Following are two fake international stories that would lend themselves to a single, compiled story. For the purposes of examining the compiled version, we will call the first one *Story A* and the second one *Story B*.

Story A:

African summit may be "decisive" for Angola

NAIROBI, Kenya (AP) — President Lothar Amin of Uganda said Friday the African summit conference on Angola next week would be decisive for Angola's world role.

He urged Africans to bury their differences concerning the war-torn nation, Uganda radio reported.

Uganda Broadcasting Corp., monitored in Nairobi, quoted Amin as saying that Angola would not be admitted to the United Nations unless the Organization of African Unity agreed to recognize a government in the former Portuguese colony, which gained independence last November.

"Angola's relationships with its neighbours are a question of immediate concern to the OAU," Amin was quoted as saying.

Amin, the president of the OAU, raised the issue of Angolan border incursions in its continuing series of civil disorders.

Story B:

Russia issues warning
to U.S. about Angola

MOSCOW (UPI) — Russia called today for an end to the military involvement in Angola by foreign powers.

"Russia comes out firmly for the termination of foreign armed intervention in Angola," the newspaper Pravda said.

"The people of Angola should be given the right to decide themselves the questions of building a new life in the conditions of peace and freedom," said the newspaper, which is often seen as the organ of official Russian policy.

Pravda said the Kremlin would restructure its arms treaties with Angola if Western nations, particularly the United States, would cease intervention in the African nation's affairs.

Russia has an estimated 500 military advisers in Angola, according to Western observers. They work with some 2,000 Cuban soldiers who have been seen fighting alongside Angolan troops.

Because these stories are both concerned with Angola, there is a rationale for combining them into one single story. Notice that the following compiled version begins with the phrase *From Wire Service Reports*, a common way to give the wire services credit for compiled stories.

Russia and Uganda eye
Angola's future in OAU

From Wire Service Reports

As African leaders prepared for next week's summit on Angola, Uganda's president said the conference would affect Angola's future, and Russia called for an end to military involvement there.

In Nairobi, Ugandan President Lothar Amin said Friday the African summit conference on Angola next week would be decisive for Angola's world role.

> He urged Africans to bury their differences concerning the war-torn nation, Uganda radio reported.
>
> Uganda Broadcasting Corp., monitored in Nairobi, quoted Amin as saying Angola would not be admitted to the United Nations unless the Organization of African Unity agreed to recognize a government in the former Portuguese colony, which gained independence in November.
>
> "Angola's relationships with its neighbours are a question of immediate concern to the OAU," Amin was quoted as saying.
>
> Amin, the president of the OAU, raised the issue of Angolan border incursions in its continuing series of civil disorders.
>
> In Moscow, Russia called for an end to the military involvement in Angola by foreign powers.
>
> "Russia comes out firmly for the termination of foreign armed intervention in Angola," the newspaper Pravda said.
>
> "The people of Angola should be given the right to decide themselves the questions of building a new life in the conditions of peace and freedom," said the newspaper, which is often seen as the organ of official Russian policy.
>
> Pravda said the Kremlin would restructure its arms treaties with Angola if Western nations, particularly the United States, would cease intervention in the African nation's affairs.
>
> Russia has an estimated 500 military advisers in Angola, according to Western observers. They work with some 2,000 Cuban soldiers who have been seen fighting alongside Angolan troops.

In the compiled version, I wrote a multiple-element lead with a short introductory phrase. I prefer not to do this, but, as is true for most multiple-element leads, the lead tends to be long-ish and slightly more complex because of the amount of information that must be included.

The lead contains information from Story A and from Story B. As a result, the reader may be confused about where information in the second paragraph is coming from. To clarify this, I use the transition *In Nairobi....*

Now that I have a transition, *I write the entire Nairobi part of the story.* When I finish the Nairobi part, I start telling the story from the Soviet Union. I need another transition here because I am switching locales, so I write *In Moscow....* Then *I write the entire Moscow part of the story.*

If we label the paragraphs according to which story their information comes from, the underlying structure of the compiled story looks like the diagram in Table 4.2.

Table 4.2 Structure of simple multiple-element story

A & B
Transition & A
A
A
A
A
A
Transition & B
B
B
B
B
B

Shirttailing

The above is an example of a multiple-element story with only two elements. But multiple-element stories often contain more than two elements. When this happens, it is easy to lose control over the organization of the story.

A simple technique called a ***shirttail*** allows you to cover a number of elements briefly without losing control over the story. Following is an example of a shirttail:

Councillors seek to limit debates

A group of legislators Tuesday agreed to limit debate in the Legislative Council in order to avoid the late-night sessions that plagued the panel last year.

Members agreed that no more than two debates should be held during a single sitting, according to Mr. Fred Li Wah Ming. Mr. Li is a member of a temporary committee studying the proposal.

> The committee also recommended that each speaker be allowed to speak for only 10 minutes on any motion, Mr. Li said. The rule would not apply to the sponsor of the motion.
>
> The total amount of time allowed for debate on a single motion would be limited to two hours.
>
> Other recommendations included these:
>
> • Complex questions requesting statistics and broad policy explanations would not be permitted;
>
> • Questions based on rumours and press reports also would not be permitted;
>
> • The chairman would be elected by members in a secret ballot;
>
> • The chairman would be empowered to cut off a person's speech if the speaker violated the rules.
>
> Mr. Li said the recommendations will be taken up by the entire Council next month.

In this story, the *shirttail* is the part of the story that itemizes the "other recommendations". As you can plainly see, this technique allows the journalist to cover a great deal of ground quickly and succinctly. The black dots that mark each paragraph are called ***bullets***. Some newspapers use dashes instead of bullets.

I chose an example from a legislative body for a specific reason: The shirttail is ideally suited for covering legislative matters, because legislatures usually make several important decisions in each sitting, and the decisions often are unrelated. Appellate courts also make several decisions in one day, and they typically are unrelated, so the technique is often invoked in court reporting.

5

Covering Speeches

Covering a speech is one of the easiest tasks for a journalist, and this is why I am taking it up early in this book.

The reason it is easy is that, when a speech is given, the journalist acts as little more than a secretary, passively taking dictation. Aside from a question or two after the speech, most journalists don't do more than this.

This is not the best way to cover a speech, but it is very typical. The best approach to covering a speech requires some foresight and preparation.

Rule No. 33:
Do not write speeches in chronological order.

One of the most common errors I see in my students' speech stories is reporting the event in chronological order. When I see phrases such as *the prime minister opened his speech with ... ; then he said ... ; next, he mentioned ... ;* and *he concluded his speech with ...* — when I see these phrases in a speech story, I assume the writer did not write the story in inverted pyramid style.

Students often think they are reporting the speech properly if they report it in chronological order. Intuitively, it seems to be the correct approach; however, prime ministers, appeals court judges, cabinet ministers — these people are not journalists. They do not know how to present information for newspaper audiences. They do not speak in inverted pyramid style. *You*, on the other hand, *are* a journalist. You should make every effort to re-package the information in a style that will be easily digested by your readers.

Preliminary Preparations

Notice of a speech usually comes to the newspaper as a press release from a sponsoring organization. Rotary Club International, for example, holds regular luncheons featuring guest speakers. Universities and colleges invite speakers from distant places.

Usually, journalists are invited to attend because the resulting news sheds favourable publicity on the sponsoring organizations.

The press release announcing a speaking engagement will contain a telephone number and the name of a contact for more information. The journalist should contact this person and confirm all the information on the release.

For a visit by a prominent person, the journalist should request the sponsoring organization for an introduction prior to the speaking engagement. A former prime minister of a foreign country, for example, might grant an interview for a profile before the speech. There's always a chance that a profile could enhance the speech story by running as a sidebar to the speech story.

The journalist also should request ***an advance copy of prepared text***. This is a typewritten copy of the speech. Some speakers prepare them, others do not. When they are made available, however, they are immensely useful in notetaking during the speech.

It goes without saying that the journalist should do research on the speaker, especially a prominent one. News accounts of the person should be reviewed; if the person has published books and articles, these should be inspected as well if time permits.

On the day of the event, the journalist should make his presence known to the speaker. Usually there is a bit of slack between the time the speaker walks into the room and the time the formalities begin. If possible, the journalist should approach the speaker during this slack time, introduce himself and his organization, and explain his purpose. Then the journalist should position himself in the audience so he is clearly visible to the speaker. Sitting in the front row is highly recommended.

The reasons for these last two actions will be clear in a moment.

When the speaker begins, the journalist should ***note the exact time*** to the nearest minute. Then, if an advance copy of prepared text has been made available, the journalist should follow the text carefully during the speech. Any deviations from the text should be carefully noted in the margins.

Applause, boos, laughter, shouts from protestors and other ***interruptions*** should be carefully noted. Six interruptions due to applause might be a valuable detail, something worth mentioning as part of the story — but the journalist will lose count if he doesn't make a note of each one.

When the speaker has finished, the journalist should note the time once again. The difference between the two times is the length of the speech in minutes. Sometimes this is another valuable detail: A major policy address delivered in 17 minutes is probably too short, but it's the journalist's duty at least to make an empirical record of the time lapse. Now, assuming that the journalist has introduced himself and positioned himself properly in the audience, the journalist will have no difficulty getting the speaker's attention during the subsequent question-and-answer period.

Likewise, if the journalist is not satisfied with the speaker's responses to questions, the journalist can quickly approach the speaker when everything is over and interview him at the podium. Prominent people often are surrounded by admirers during this time, so the journalist will have difficulty making eye contact with the speaker if he has not already introduced himself. This is a time when high dividends are paid to aggressive reporters.

Expected Information

Applause, boos, shouts from protestors — all of these should be mentioned in your speech story if they seem significant. Your editors will expect this information in your stories.

Other information that is commonly expected are: (1) the location of the event; (2) the sponsors of the event; and (3) the title of the speech.

This is relatively unimportant information, however, so it should not be placed high in the story. I recommend that it be provided in the concluding paragraph, where it can easily be cut:

> The prime minister made his comments in a speech titled "Regional Modernization" at the dedication of a new containerized terminal port at Shek O. The event was sponsored by the Port Authority.

In any event, *do not* place this information in Paragraph 2 or Paragraph 3 unless such information is especially noteworthy. If a Jewish organization invites a Palestinian leader to speak, then this is noteworthy.

Handling Quotations

One problem that arises from prepared texts is that speakers deviate from them. The journalist should keep careful marginal notes indicating ***deviations from prepared text***. If the journalist wants to use these quotes, he should do so; after all, they are just as much a part of the speech as the rest of the material.

At such times, journalists will note that a speaker's comments were made this way:

> In a departure from his prepared remarks, the prime minister issued a note of caution about the breakup of the Baltic states.
>
> "The number of nations with significant military capability has nearly doubled in the past decade," he said.

The reason the journalist tells the reader that this is a deviation from prepared text is that they are *more spontaneous*. They are probably a clearer view of the prime minister's personal position on the issue rather than the position of speechwriters and policymakers who assisted him in preparing his remarks.

One of the most common questions I get from students is whether or not they can use ***quotes from the question-and-answer session*** as part of the main speech story. The answer is yes, but it is appropriate to indicate to the reader how the remarks were made:

> In a question-and-answer session after the speech, the prime minister said....

Indeed, if remarks made after the ***Q-A session*** are more important than the rest of the speech itself, the journalist should feel no hesitation in building an entire story around the comments made *after* the speech — assuming there is enough material to write about, of course. The rationale behind this is that the speaker is a public figure, and he is making remarks in a public forum before representatives of the press. In other words, everything is ***on the record***, or in the public domain for everyone to see. Hence, if he makes a significant statement, it should be reported in the press.

Types of Quotations

There are many ways to tell the reader what the speaker said. There are direct quotes, partial quotes, paraphrases, and extended quotes, to name a few.

Direct quotes, which are illustrated in the section below on attribution, require quotation marks. By using quotation marks, the journalist implies that the material between the quotes is precisely what the speaker said.

There are two common caveats to this basic principle: One is that *journalists tend to "clean up" a person's quotes.* The other is that, when translating from another language, the words inside the quotes are obviously not what was said, because it was spoken in another language.

To ***clean up*** a person's quotes is to remove the stuttering — the *ah*'s and the *uh*'s and the *mmm*'s — that is, the grunts and murmurs that add little to the quote and look silly in print. Indeed, journalists go further than this, actually improving on the grammar of people who are speaking spontaneously in interviews. The rationale is that no one speaks perfectly, and sometimes small grammatical mistakes make speakers look stupid — when they really are not stupid at all. Naturally, however, it is inappropriate to change a quote so much that the meaning is altered.

Regarding foreign languages, to translate a foreign language literally into English often is bizarre and meaningless. The journalist should translate in such a way as to capture the meaning of the speaker's remarks in idiomatic English, if at all possible. *Furthermore, the journalist who is interviewing a subject in English for an English-language publication should take notes in English, not his native language.* The reason is that, by the time the writing begins, there will have been two translations, and some of the meaning may have been altered.

One way to avoid the translation problem is to paraphrase the speaker. A ***paraphrase*** is a restatement of the speaker's comments in your own words. Usually, a paraphrase will be a shorter statement, a summary of what was said. There are no quotation marks, and it uses different phrases, different words. If it is impossible to paraphrase without using the speaker's exact words, then a direct quotation should be used instead.

A paraphrase is one kind of indirect quotation. An ***indirect quotation*** is one that recasts the speaker's words in another way and eliminates the quotation marks.

Extended quotes are lengthy, word-for-word direct quotations of a speaker's comments, and they often are provided by newspapers that cover heads of state during momentous occasions. Newspapers that provide this kind of extended coverage develop reputations as ***newspapers of record*** because they provide a semi-official record of major government proceedings.

Figure 5.1 Types of quotes

Direct quotation:

"The government and the people of Hong Kong have an imperative moral responsibility to assist China in its drive toward modernization," Dr. Zhou said.

Indirect quotation:

Hong Kong and its people have the responsibility to aid China in its modernization efforts, Dr. Zhou said.

Partial quote:

Hong Kong and its people have "an imperative moral responsibility" to aid China in its modernization efforts, Dr. Zhou said.

Paraphrase:

Hong Kong should help China catch up to the modern world, Dr. Zhou said.

Extended quotes are possible only if there is a prepared text, or if the speech was tape recorded and transcribed.

The extended quotation does not require quotation marks, and there is only one statement of attribution. This should precede the quoted material. Here is an example:

> Following is the complete text of the prime minister's remarks:
>
> Members of Parliament, guests, ladies and gentlemen of the press, it is a sombre occasion that brings us together this morning....

Occasionally, when quoting a person at some length, the journalist desires to delete material that is irrelevant to the central theme of the story. This is done with the ***ellipsis***, which is three stops in a row (...). In the quotation from the prime minister above, there is an ellipsis after "morning". The reason that there are four full stops is that the ellipsis is followed by the full stop that ends the sentence itself. In the above example, if an ellipsis were inserted after "Members of Parliament", then it would have to include the comma, like this:

> Following is the complete text of the prime minister's remarks:
> Members of Parliament ... , it is a sombre occasion that brings us together this morning....

Attribution

The technique that journalists use to identify a person speaking in a news story is called ***attribution***. This chapter introduces several techniques for attribution.

The most common way to attribute full, direct quotations is to place the attribution at the end of the quote:

> The majority of the board favoured the proposal for a new emergency dialing system, which is expected to cost approximately $1.5 million.
>
> "I am concerned about the cost of this system. However, I believe that the initial capital outlay will be offset by savings in salaries at a later date," said Mrs. Gloria de la Cruz, who represents the Central District.

Placing attribution at the end of a quotation poses no problem in speech stories, because there is only one speaker; when the reader sees an open quote, he knows who the speaker is.

There is a slight problem when there is more than one individual quoted in the story, however. The problem is that, if several people are participating in the discussion — the usual case when it comes to board meetings — the reader will be confused about the identity of the speaker until the end of the quotation.

Rule No. 42:
Introduce your speakers.

A minimal solution is to introduce the speaker with a *transitional paragraph*, like this:

> The majority of the board favoured the proposal for a new emergency dialing system, which is expected to cost approximately $1.5 million.
>
> Among those favouring the proposal was Mrs. Gloria de la Cruz, who represents the Central District.
>
> "I am concerned about the cost of this system. However, I believe that the initial capital outlay will be offset by savings in salaries at a later date," said Mrs. de la Cruz.

Notice that the quotation stands alone as a separate paragraph. This is a common journalistic practice.

As mentioned above, insertion of a transitional paragraph is a minimal solution to the attribution problem. A better solution would be to move the attribution as well, like this:

> The majority of the board favoured the proposal for a new emergency dialing system, which is expected to cost approximately $1.5 million.
>
> Among those favouring the proposal was Mrs. Gloria de la Cruz, who represents the Central District.
>
> "I am concerned about the cost of this system," said Mrs. de la Cruz. "However, I believe that the initial capital outlay will be offset by savings in salaries at a later date."

This is better because it provides rhythm to the writing, and rhythm plays an important role in the mental processes of the reader. If there is a general rule, it is this: *When a quotation runs for two or more sentences, the attribution should be placed after the first sentence.* This is known as ***embedded attribution***.

The rule may be applied to longer sentences which begin with extended phrases, and to compound sentences, like this:

> "Being a firm advocate of social programmes," Mrs. de la Cruz said, "I willingly cast my vote in favour of this measure."

> Councillor Li Ka Shing immediately threw in his support.
>
> "I also support such programmes," he said, "and I join my distinguished colleague in casting my vote in favour of the proposal."

Indirect quotations may be handled in the same fashion:

> As an advocate of social programmes, the councillor said, she willingly supported the measure.

One final note on rhythm: Whether the writer chooses *said Mrs. de la Cruz* or *Mrs. de la Cruz said* is largely irrelevant. Both are correct. However, the first one is more rhythmic and might be preferred by some writers. In any case, the rhythm of a short phrase such as this is driven partly by the larger context, so a good choice requires a feel for the rhythm of surrounding sentences. For more on rhythm in writing, see Chapter 7.

Another factor that influences the placement of *said* around the quotation is the length of the speaker's organizational title. If a speaker's title is very long, then *said* must come first, and the speaker's name may be followed by either a comma or a colon, like this:

> Said Hong Kong Tourist Association Director Harold Smith: "Hong Kong is now the No. 1 tourist destination in Asia, and the only way we can keep that lead is to treat our visitors as guests."

Inverting the word order of the attributive phrase like this, and following it with a colon, has been popularized by *Time* magazine, which frequently does this.

Using Punctuation Around Quotation Marks

In general, a statement inside quotation marks is called a ***direct quotation***, and the phrase implies that the words are the exact words of the speaker. ***Double quotes*** are preferred, although ***single quotes*** are acceptable to some publishers.[1] If you use double quotes for direct quotations, then you should

[1] The British book publishing industry makes heavy use of single quotes for direct quotations; however, the British newspaper industry prefers double quotes, as do all sectors of the American publishing industry.

use single quotes for quotations within quotations. Here are some examples of how quotes may be used with other punctuation marks:

Simple direct quotes, with punctuation inside quotation marks:

> "He is not going," she said.
>
> He responded by fidgeting with his watch. Finally he said, "I'm sorry to hear this."

Simple, direct quotes, with embedded attribution:

> "I hate to say this," she said, "but I cannot in good conscience support this resolution."

Figure 5.2 illustrates some alternatives for punctuating around quoted matter. One thing you should keep in mind when looking at Figure 5.2 is that the past tense — *said* in this case — is preferred. Use the present tense only if you can justify it, as in a hard chronology, for example.

Also *said* is preferred to most other attributive words. This is discussed below.

Figure 5.2 Punctuation and Attribution

All of the following are acceptable. Note especially the use of the colon when: (1) the attribution precedes the quote; and (2) when the word order is inverted. *Time* magazine relies heavily on this technique.

Says he: "...."	"... ," said he.
He says, "...."	"... ," says he.
Said he: "...."	"... ," he says.
He said, "...."	"... ," he said.
"... ," he said, "...."	"... ," he says, "...."

Running quotations are quotes that continue for more than one paragraph. Note that there are no close quotes until the final paragraph. Using close quotes before the end of a running quote is a very common error:

> "I hate to say this," she said, "but I cannot in good conscience support this resolution.
>
> "The matter has only just been brought up before the Council, and there has been insufficient public debate on this issue.
>
> "For these reasons, Mr. Chairman, I abstain, and with this, I conclude my remarks."

Quotes within quotes require single quotes inside double quotes:

> "The Governor yelled, 'Get out!' when aides brought up the matter of his affair with Miss Thomson," the counsellor said.

Using the Colon

The colon is a refreshing departure from the routine way of linking quotes to attribution with a comma. The technique is illustrated in Figure 5.2.

The traditional method of attribution places a comma between the quote and the attribution, but here is an example of doing attribution with a colon:

> WASHINGTON — A young woman called, a publicist: "Taki thought you might want to know what he looks like."[2]

This is grammatically correct: The colon often is used at the end of a sentence that is followed by explanatory material, such as this sentence. When you use this style, the material following the colon should be capitalized if it is an independent clause, but it should not be capitalized if it is merely a phrase.

The most common way to use the colon around attribution is illustrated by *Time* magazine. *Time* relies heavily on the colon for attribution. Usually, it takes this style:

> Tokyo's Shigeo Shimoda, 48, has worked most of his adult life for Matsushita Electric Industrial Co. Ltd., one of Japan's most powerful firms. He usually does not arrive home until long after the children have gone to bed.
>
> Says Shimoda: "My hobby is my work."

Note that the word order is inverted in the attribution. Normally, the verb follows the subject in a declarative sentence in English, but it does not in this case.

When the word order is inverted, then a colon is required. If the word order had been normal, then a comma would have been required: *Shimoda says, "My hobby is my work."*

---

[2] This story appears in full in Chapter 8.

Be careful in using the inverted word order and colon as your form of attribution: It quickly becomes *overworked* — that is, it looks hackneyed if it is used too much.

"Said", "Uttered" or "Averred"?

Some beginning writers squirm when "said" appears more than twice in a story chockablock with direct quotes.

To ease the discomfort, they resort to alternatives: *uttered, averred, conceded, muttered, claimed, insisted, asserted, divulged, told, answered, mentioned, remarked, announced, expressed, declaimed, declared, related, commented, observed, replied, retorted, rejoined, concurred....*

Rule No. 34:
Use said for attribution.

Unfortunately, the full list of attributive verbs is about three times longer than this, but the point is made: There is no reason to resort to these words. "Said" is an invisible word, like "the". No one complains that a writer used "the" too many times. It is not a "noisy" word.

Words like "uttered" and "averred" are exceptionally noisy, and when the writer uses more than one of them, it causes enormous static. These words should be avoided except for those instances when they suit the way a quotation specifically was uttered, muttered, sputtered or blubbered, but only if sputtering and murmuring are related to the news event.

One that bothers me a lot and that shows up frequently in students' work is *laughed*: "I got married when I was 18," he laughed. Problem is that people laugh before and after speaking, but they cannot *laugh words*. You should write ... *he said, laughing*.

Tape Recorders

It must be a truism that beginning writers love tape recorders. They lug them around like security blankets, but they are not necessary for routine news coverage.

Figure 5.3 lists advantages and disadvantages of recorders. In a recent study of American journalists, only one-third said they regularly use tape recorders; the other two-thirds did not think recorders were worth the bother.

Figure 5.3 Advantages and Disadvantages of Tape Recorders

Advantages:

1. The quotations are exact, even down to the "ahs" and "uhs".

Disadvantages:

1. They cost more than pencils and paper.
2. They are one more piece of gear to lug around.
3. The sound may be poor without a good microphone properly positioned.
4. Some speakers object to tape recorders, but not to notetaking.
5. The tape will have to be turned over during a long speech or interview.
6. The batteries may run down or the electric cord or the microphone cord may be kicked out accidentally.
7. The journalist should take notes anyway in the event of one of the above mishaps.
8. The existence of audio tapes invites subpoenas in the event a legal dispute arises from the news event.
9. All the quotations are in a linear order.

Final score: 9-1 against.

The biggest disadvantage is probably the last one — the fact that all the quotations are in linear order. The significance of this will be lost on the novice, but he will quickly learn its significance when he begins to write a story based on tape recorded information. If all the quotes are in linear order, then the journalist must rewind and fastforward the tape several times while writing the story. This can be extremely time consuming — not to mention frustrating.

Some journalists try to avoid this problem by jotting down the tape counter number for selected quotes. But the journalist cannot predict which quotes will be most useful when the time comes to write the story. Besides, jotting down the counter number is distracting: The journalist should be listening to the speaker and taking notes, not watching the counter. Not to mention that the journalist many times will be forced to leave the tape recorder in an place where it is inconvenient to watch the counter — on a podium or a low coffee table, for example — and will not be able to see the counter.

Because notes should be taken anyway in the event of equipment failure, it is better to develop notetaking skills and rely on them. The tape recorder should be used as a backup only.

The Say-Nothing Lead

One of the most common blunders that beginners make is to write what I call the ***say-nothing lead***. This was discussed in Chapter 3, but it is worth repeating here because it usually appears in speech stories. In a speech story, it is a lead with little or no substance. It doesn't say much. This is what it looks like: "So-and-so gave a speech on such-and-such." There are variations, but they all have this basic structure.

Following are four examples of say-nothing leads written by four of my journalism students covering the same speech:

> HONG KONG — The president of the Chinese Academy of Sciences gave a speech on the 42nd congregation at Sir Run Run Shaw Hall in The Chinese University of Hong Kong Thursday.
>
> HONG KONG — A prominent Mainland Chinese scientist spoke before 400 guests at The Chinese University of Hong Kong on Thursday. He spoke about the modernization of China.
>
> HONG KONG — A prominent Chinese physicist made a speech about scientific and technological development of China at The Chinese University of Hong Kong on Thursday.
>
> HONG KONG — A prominent Chinese scientist delivered a speech at Chinese University of Hong Kong Thursday, concerning unity of all for China's modernization.

All of these statements are true, but they are not summary leads because they don't summarize what the speaker said. The real lead was buried in each case.

This was the real story:

> HONG KONG — The leaders of Hong Kong have a "historic and moral imperative" to promote the modernization of China, one of the Mainland's most eminent physicists said Thursday.

This was rather strong language from the man who could rightly be called China's top scientist. The difference between this lead and the say-nothing leads above is that this lead summarizes the speaker's main point. To write "a certain person spoke on a certain topic" does not summarize the main point of the speech.

Identifying the Main Point

Beginning writers are often confused about identifying the main point of a speech. Here are two common problems:

- Some speakers make several points of equal merit.
- Other speakers develop a point of view that does not seem newsworthy, and meantime they allude to something that seems very newsworthy, but they do so without developing the idea very much.

In the first case, the journalist is forced to pick one for the lead and develop it in the story. If the other points must be mentioned, they can either be *shirttailed*, a technique explained in Chapter 4, or handled like the so-called "problem" speech illustrated below.

In the second case, the writer should not feel constrained to emphasize the same points as the speaker. The writer has journalistic licence to focus on whatever point appears to be the most newsworthy. After all, the writer is the journalist, not the speaker, so the journalist establishes the agenda for the news media.

The "Problem" Speech

Occasionally a speaker "jumps around" too much, making it difficult for the journalist to write a well organized piece developing a single line of thought. This happens in personal interviews as well. And there are times when the various points covered are all significant and worth reporting.

When this happens, journalists sometimes itemize the points with a shirttail.

This method is illustrated again in the following excerpt from the *International Herald Tribune*:

Japan's New Finance Czar No Longer Sees U.S. as Model[3]

By James Sterngold
New York Times Service

1 TOKYO — Japan is charting a course that is dramatically independent of the United States, the nation's top international finance official said Wednesday.

2 In a speech at Tokyo University, Mr. Tadao Chino said that the United States' former position as a role model for Japan is no longer appropriate.

3 "The United States once was the model of success that Japan had to learn from," he recalled. Now, however, Mr. Chino, 57, takes a far different view of the country he once idolized.

4 He is the newly appointed vice minister of finance for international affairs, which makes him the top financial policy maker for the world's largest creditor nation.

5 He promised to chart a course that is defiantly independent from the United States.

6 Mr. Chino indicated that Japan would become even more assertive in pushing its financial objectives, whether in the World Bank, among the Group of Seven industrial democracies or in trade negotiations with the United States.

7 Mr. Chino is at the head of a generation of Japanese that reshaped Japan's international financial policy, much as the Ministry of International Trade and Industry developed and implemented Japan's industrial strategy.

8 In his speech, Mr. Chino outlined a range of issues on which Japan intended to exert its considerable financial influence, among them the following:

---

[3] *International Herald Tribune*, Hong Kong, Tuesday, 6 August 1991, No. 33728, p. 9.

9 • He insisted that the *keiretsu*, Japan's groupings of industrial companies, had many positive features and that Japan was unlikely to bend to American demands that they be changed. Mr. Chino disputed assertions by U.S. trade negotiators that they exclude foreign competition and engage in unfair practices.

10 • He said he would fight the U.S. policy of forgiving some of the debt of friendly countries, like Poland and Egypt.

11 • He said the Russia would receive no financial aid from Japan until it clarified the relationship between the Central government and the republics, reformed its economy, returned a group of northern islands seized from Japan in the waning days of World War II, and reduced its military presence in Asia.

12 • He said that while Japan would contribute aid to Eastern Europe, it was more interested in Asian countries as a low-cost manufacturing base.

13 In the Japanese system, the finance minister is a political appointee. The vice minister....

Annotations to *finance czar*

In ***Paragraph 1***, the writer places the speaker's most important idea without fully identifying the speaker by name. This is because most readers would not know who Mr. Chino is.

Paragraph 2 identifies him fully by name and adds a bit more information, so it expands and supports the lead, as a supporting graf should.

Paragraph 4 establishes the speaker's authority.

Because the speech lacks focus, a shirttail begins in ***Paragraph 9***. It is preceded by a colon at the end of the previous paragraph, and each element in the itemization is denoted with a bullet.

The shirttail is ***Paragraphs 10–12***. Each element in the itemization begins with "He said". This makes the items parallel in structure and strengthens the relationship between them. Also, there are no transitions within the shirttail: The bullets make it clear that the speaker is jumping from subject to subject.

6

Interviewing Techniques

The importance of interviews in journalism is a given. If there were axioms in journalism, two of them would be these: (1) a reporter is only as good as the information he gets — and (2) most of this information comes from talking to other people, his ***sources***.

But interviewing plays an important role in other fields too — law, psychiatry and business, for example. Even the social sciences — psychology, sociology, anthropology — rely on interviews for collection of information about people and cultures.

In light of its importance in academic fields, it should come as no surprise that a person can fill a shelf with books on interviewing techniques. Some techniques, such as the methods for collecting public opinion data, are highly stylized. So most books on the subject are tailored to meet the needs of scholars in specific fields. Journalism has its share of the titles.

So there is enough written on the subject that it is worth summarizing the main points as a separate chapter. This chapter is placed before the chapter on personality profiles for a good reason: The interview will play a pivotal role in the success or failure of writing a personality profile, so the journalist should be fully prepared to conduct interviews properly. In preparing an interview, the journalist should think about all the questions he or she wants answers to. For this reason, we will spend some time examining *types of questions*.

Taxonomy of Question Types

A ***taxonomy*** is a technique for classifying things. In interviewing, there are ways of classifying questions.

The first way of classifying questions — and probably the most common one — is as open-ended and closed-ended. A ***closed-ended*** question limits the possible responses of the interviewee. Example:

> "Would you say that you agree or disagree with the president's arms reduction policy?"

The respondent ostensibly has only two options — to agree or to disagree. The question is considered *highly closed-ended* because it severely restricts the responses. A question that provides only two possible answers is also called a ***bipolar question***.

Closed-ended questions can provide many more options. A film critic might ask a film director, "What films come to mind when I mention Antonioni?" A question like this is *moderately closed-ended.*

The advantage of closed-ended questions is that they permit the journalist quickly to get specific information. The disadvantage is that they limit the amount and kind of information obtained.

The open-ended question, on the other hand, will broaden the discussion. An ***open-ended*** question imposes few restrictions on the interviewee. Answers are longer, and the information may be richer. Examples:

> "Tell me about yourself."
> "How do you feel about marriage?"
> "What was your childhood like?"

All of these are *highly open-ended.*

Questions may be *moderately open-ended*, such as: "Why is Turgenev your favourite author?" "How do you account for Buckminster Fuller's influence on your work?"

Questions may be classified also as primary and secondary. A ***primary question*** opens up a new area of discussion. It may have a transition, such as the following: "Turning now to your education, I understand that you spent two years at L'Ecole des Beaux Arts in Paris. Is that correct?"

A ***secondary question*** elicits additional information about the facts established with the primary questions: "Did you experience any formative influences during your Paris years?"

There are other types of questions — leading questions, probes, clearinghouse probes, and so on. They will be taken up below.

Interviewing Techniques

With a classification scheme established, it is possible now to formulate some interviewing techniques.

The most common interviewing techniques are directive and nondirective. A ***directive interview*** is a series of closed-ended questions:

Q. What time did the first call come into police headquarters?

A. The first call came in at 2048 hours.

Q. What was the nature of the call?

A. The caller complained that she heard gunshots from the direction of the shopping arcade.

Q. The caller was a woman?

A. Yes.

Q. What's her name?

A. I can't give you that information. She's a prospective witness.

Q. Did she say how many shots she heard?

A. She said it sounded like rapid-fire, like an automatic weapon.

Notice the locus of control. Here, the journalist has complete control over the direction of the conversation. This is the most significant attribute of the directive technique. As in this example, the directive technique is highly favoured for eliciting specific information quickly. Spot news events usually require this approach.

In the nondirective interview, the locus of control is passed to the interviewee. This is because the ***nondirective interview*** is a series of open-ended questions:

Q. When you first arrived in Manila, what happened?

A. Well, I reported for work immediately. One of the bank's vice-presidents, Leonard Sabiaga, took me on a tour of all the departments. He was pleasant and courteous, but I sensed some coolness toward him everywhere we went in the downtown office.

Q. You say you sensed some coolness toward him. Could you be more specific?

A. You know, when you walk into a room and everyone is smiling and talking, and suddenly they fall silent and the smiles fade. That sort of thing.

Q. What do you attribute this to?

A. In retrospect, I believe that the word had gotten out that he was under investigation by the banking authorities. There were rumours and allegations. Being new to the organization, I was unfamiliar with the investigation, and all of this came as a surprise to me when it broke in the Manila papers just a few days later.

In the above example, the interviewee has much more control in leading the conversation. Also, the second question is referred to as a ***probe*** or ***follow-up question***. It is designed to elicit more information about a point made by the interviewee.

There are several special types of probes — the nudging probe, the reflexive probe, the summary probe, and the clearinghouse probe.

The ***nudging probe*** is an inducement to continue talking:

"Go on."
"Please continue."

Sometimes journalists know that an interviewee's facts are incorrect. When this situation arises, the reflexive probe is a tactful way to draw out the correct information. The ***reflexive probe*** is a question that asks the interviewee to reconsider a statement that appears to be factually inacurrate:

"You mean the 1992 elections, don't you?"
"Did you say 'million' or 'billion'?"

There are times when the journalist wants to recapitulate the main points. This may be because the journalist wants to be certain he has all the facts correctly — or it may be a way to give the subject an opportunity to change his mind or expand on a point for the purpose of clarification. For this purpose, there is the ***mirror probe***, a question that summarizes a series of answers:

"I want to make sure I've got this straight: You came to Manila because of the salary offer and because it was difficult to make a career move in New Zealand because of the employment situation. Is that right?"

Finally, the ***clearinghouse probe*** is a sweeping question designed to draw out any additional related material that may have been inadvertently skipped:

> "Is there anything else you can remember about your first days in Manila that might be relevant?"

Now, a skillful interviewer can combine these types of questions in the funnel technique. The ***funnel technique*** is *the process of gradually narrowing the focus of the interview from a general focus to a very specific one*. A profile about an individual who has had a very controversial past obviously would want to address some of the controversies; however, it would be offputting to the subject to be confronted with these at the outset of the interview.

In a situation such as this, the journalist should begin discussion with a series of open-ended questions that would enable the subject to broach these issues himself. Failing that, the journalist could gradually narrow the focus with a series of probes, perhaps, or some closed-ended questions.

Another way to classify questions is as objective, subjective and indeterminate.

An ***objective question*** is a question that may be answered with observable characteristics. These are things like names, dates, places, and so on. Examples:

> "When you arrived in Kuching, how did you get from the airport to the hotel?"

> "Where did you meet Mr. Tiburcio?"

A ***subjective question*** is one that elicits opinions or feelings:

> "How did you feel about moving out to Kyoto after 10 years in the downtown Tokyo office?"

> "What do you think about the American embargo on prisoner-made goods from China?"

An ***indeterminate question*** is one that elicits neither opinion or observable characteristics, but leaves the type of answer up to the subject:

> "Tell me about your career at Mitsubishi."

> "Can you give me some idea what life is like for a Portugese expatriate in Macau?"

The indeterminate question is the most neutral, so it is an effective way to elicit a broad response while preserving the journalistic values of fairness, balance and objectivity.

Regardless of the types of questions to be asked, the journalist should have a fairly clear idea where he wants the conversation to go. For this reason, it is wise to have an ***interview schedule***, which is little more than a list of questions.

I used to keep my interview schedules on the last page of my reporter's notebook, where I could refer to it quickly. During lapses in the conversation or notetaking, I would discretely flip to the last page and check off all of the answered questions and see what questions remained unanswered.

Leading Questions

One problem journalists face is phrasing a question so that the expected response is suggested by the question. Skilled politicians often recognize this and accuse journalists of unfairness. This could be embarrassing to a journalist if done during a press conference with all of his journalistic colleagues looking on.

Here is an example of a question that anticipates the response:

> "You don't agree with the management's decision on this, do you?"

This question suggests that the journalist expects the interviewee to say, "No, I don't agree with management on this."

Another problem is the so-called ***hidden premise***. If you don't know whether a person is married or not, and you ask:

> "Will your wife be joining you in Brunei?"

Then you have employed a hidden premise. This question presumes that the subject is married, but the subject's marital status should first be established.

When the expected response or hidden premises are included in a question, then the journalist is asking a ***leading question***. Here is an example:

> "You do remember, don't you, that the board of directors put down $2 million in securities to buy 40 percent of the shipping firm?"

Research has shown that leading questions tend to elicit distorted information. And sophisticated interviewees will recognize leading questions for what they are and berate the journalist.

Encouragements and Nonverbal Cues

Some interviewees are shy. Some are uncooperative. They may need encouragement.

Encouragements are affirmative responses by the interviewer. Examples:

> "That's interesting."
> "Uh-huh."
> "I understand."
> "Mm-hmmm."

Encouragements serve several purposes. They indicate that the journalist is interested in the responses, that the journalist is listening, and that the journalist would like the interviewee to continue.

At times, the lack of encouragements actually inhibits the interviewee, so the journalist should be conscientious about providing them if he wants the subject to continue.

The journalist should be careful about influencing the direction of the responses, however. Expressions such as "I agree" or "Good" indicate that the journalist supports the interviewee's point of view. Such behaviour is inappropriate. The journalist should remain neutral.

A ***pregnant pause*** is an awkward silence during an interview. Beginning journalists find this unnerving. Here is a typical error made by inexperienced interviewers:

> Journalist: "Tell me about your childhood."
> (Brief pause while subject ponders question.)
> Journalist: "Did you grow up in Singapore?

In the above example, the journalist asks an open-ended question at the subject, but the subject does not respond immediately. Uncomfortable with this brief silence, the journalist fills the void by asking a closed-ended question. Naturally, this discourages the subject from talking at length.

Beginners commit a similar error by injecting a comment in the middle of an interviewee's response, like this:

Q. Tell me about your childhood.
A. I was the eldest of 11 children ... (pause).
Q. You had a lot of responsibility then?

Silences should not be broken by the journalist. There are exceptions to this principle, of course. Research indicates that long silences — 10 or more seconds — are unproductive and *should* be broken by the journalist. The journalist also should take advantages of pauses if he or she wants to change the direction of the conversation, open up a new line of questioning.

Aside from waiting out the silences, journalists engage in other types of nonverbal behaviour as well. A steady gaze at the subject and a friendly expression tend to elicit fuller responses. Many journalists nod their heads while taking notes and change their facial expressions to indicate understanding or approval.

Also, the physical appearance of the journalist will give the interviewee many cues about the journalist's background and status. Within reasonable limits, the journalist should appear and behave in a manner that reflects the background and social status of his subjects.

A journalist who appears at a construction site in a dark blue suit to discuss a labour dispute with union leaders will be looked upon as an outsider. It would be difficult for him to collect information under such circumstances.

Similarly, a journalist who enters the offices of a university chancellor for an interview wearing a polo shirt and windbreaker will not be taken as seriously as his better dressed counterparts.

In preparing for any interview, the journalist should consider the social effects of his attire and dress accordingly.

Proxemics

Social scientists have clearly established that people communicate better when the spatial relationships in their environment meet their expectations.

The study of the effect of spatial relationships on communication behaviour is called ***proxemics***.

When people are too close to us, we feel a bit uncomfortable talking to them. When we see people we recognize at a distance of 15 metres, we may not say hello, but we will say hello when they reach a distance of 5 metres, for example.

When interviewing people, the journalist should be sensitive to the proxemics. For example, a journalist should never touch a subject unless the subject touches him first.

In general, it is always best to interview someone while facing him directly. Placing one's body at a slight angle to the subject can be very offputting to the subject.

Also, when sitting at a rectangular table, it is best to sit directly opposite the subject, not at one side. Social scientists have learned that sitting beside the subject on the same side of the table, or sitting on a side that is perpendicular to the side the subject is sitting on, is a sign of intimacy. This may make the subject feel uncomfortable.

Finally, the journalist should attempt to keep his eyes at the same level as the subject's eyes. To stand while interviewing someone who is sitting will make the subject uncomfortable. The reverse is true as well: Never sit while interviewing someone who is standing.

Follow-Up Interviews and Photo Sessions

When planning a personality profile, the journalist should make it clear to the subject that more than one interview may be necessary to complete the story.

This will prepare the subject for a second, or ***follow-up***, interview. At this time, the journalist should clarify all details and ask additional questions.

This is an excellent time for the ***photo session***, which is the time when all the photographs are taken. The subject will know the journalist by now, and presumably will be more relaxed. Also, the photographer will be able to take more naturalistic photographs if the journalist interviews the subject while the photographs are taken. The conversation will distract the subject, so the facial expressions will be less posed and rigid.

Rules of the Road

Sometimes people are willing to talk to journalists as long as they are not quoted in the news. Other times, they might not mind being quoted, as long as their names do not appear in the news.

In order to maintain working relationships with sources with such reservations, journalists have developed some ***rules of the road***, or procedural codes for conducting interviews under delicate conditions.

The rules have names — on-the-record, off-the-record, not-for-attribution, and background.

Most conversations are ***on-the-record***, so you are familiar already with this rule. It means that everything said in an interview may be used as fully attributed quotations in the news.

Off-the-record means just the opposite — nothing may be used under any circumstances. When a source *goes off the record* with a journalist, the journalist is expected to maintain the strictest confidence. He is expected not to divulge the information to anyone, including colleagues, spouses and editors. The information is a deeply held secret.

Not-for-attribution means that a source does not mind being quoted as long as the material is not attributed to him. Journalists use the expression "anonymous source" to attribute such information: *China is planning to increase its rhetoric against British Foreign Office proposals to democratize Hong Kong, anonymous sources in Beijing said Monday.*

Background is information provided to journalists in order to help them understand events in a broader context. The information may not be quoted, but it may be used to develop new information from other sources. It also may be used in opinion pieces, such as editorials — not as the views of the original source, but as the views of the journalist.

Ethical Concerns

The rules of the road provide some ethical problems. For example, many sources, and even some journalists, are not familiar with the fine distinctions made above. For this reason, *it is incumbent on the journalist to make it clear under which conditions the interview is being conducted.*

A likely way to do this, if there were any doubt, would be to say, "I assume that everything we talk about is on the record. Do you agree?"

If there is any question about the significance of this, then the journalist should explain its significance. If the source objects, then the journalist might explain some of the alternatives, if he wants to proceed with the interview.

Occasionally something like this happens: After a long interview that becomes increasingly unsavoury for a source, the source says, "In retrospect, I think everything I have said should be off the record."

The journalist must decide how to handle such information based on the context. If the source is sophisticated about dealings with journalists — if he is a prominent politician or diplomat, for example — then the journalist should insist that everything be kept on the record, everything that has been said. People who are less sophisticated about dealings with the press may be given the benefit of the doubt.

Another kind of problem arises with off-the-record information. Some slick politicians will go off the record in a conversation and then tell the journalist false or misleading information. Because the journalist cannot ethically use the information in any way, he cannot verify it or prove it false, except by indirect means. This may mislead him for some time.

Another ploy is for a politician to pretend to draw a journalist into his confidence by going off the record with information that is common knowledge. This may obligate the journalist to be cooperative with the source in future dealings.

In view of the ethical concerns with going off the record, some journalists make it a regular practice never to conduct interviews under such circumstances. To them, everything is on the record.

Press Conferences

When a press conference is being planned, the organizers say they are *calling* a press conference. Press conferences are never called by the press, but always by someone else — usually a prominent person or an organization.

A press conference is somewhat like a cross between a speech and an interview, the main difference being that there is only one source and several journalists — sometimes scores of journalists.

Usually, the speaker makes a brief statement and then *opens* the conference to questions. There may be a press release that accompanies the statement, and, as often as not, there is a table at the back of the room displaying press releases and supporting documents for the press to collect for their reports.

After my first few press conferences, I developed a rather cynical view of the process. For one thing, a press conference is called mainly because a person or an organization desires to impose its views on the public, and it is using the mass media to achieve this goal. The event may be elaborately "stage-managed" — that is, the presenters will be well prepared to answer tough questions with ambiguous responses — so the press conference is really a one-sided affair. Second, many journalists, seeking to impress their colleagues with the depth of their knowledge on the subject, precede their questions with elaborate expositions of their understanding of the situation. This usually begs the question, and the really basic questions go unasked.

Rule No. 10:
Ask the most basic questions that come to mind.

My experience at press conferences suggests that everyone is afraid of looking stupid by asking basic questions. For this reason, the basic questions are overlooked. Therefore, you should ask the most basic questions that come to mind.

A ***follow-up question*** is one that attempts to clarify details provided in a response to a previous question. Some journalists make it clear from the outset that they intend to ask a follow-up question, and this usually guarantees a more elaborate response.

The way to do this is to make a statement such as the following: *"Sir, I have a question, and I would like to follow it with another one, with your permission...."*

7

Feature Writing

Feature stories take many forms, but they have one common attribute: Their success as news stories rides more on the writing than on events.

Consider stories with headlines like these: "Gorbachev Threatens to Quit if Union Breaks Up," "Greek Cruise Ship Sinks in Rough Seas Off South Africa," "313 Die in Nightclub Fire in China."

These stories do not depend on brilliant writing for readership. The writing can be atrocious, but the events are newsworthy. Readers will stay with the story just to get the facts.

This is not the case with these: "Pele of Footbag Kicks Simple Sport Into High Gear," "British Inventor Builds Throwback for Hurling Hogs."

These stories depend heavily on the quality of the writing for their success — and this poses an enormous challenge to the writer.

There are many types of features, including news features, personality profiles, interviews, colour stories, how-to stories, and self-help pieces.

This chapter includes examples of a news feature and a colour story. An example of a personality profile appears in Chapter 8.

The first problem facing the feature writer is *how to start the story* — that is, finding the right peg or angle. For this reason, this chapter gives many examples of featurized leads. In reading these examples, keep in mind that the classifications of leads are not mutually exclusive. For example, a suspended interest lead might also be classified as an anecdotal lead.

News Features

Feature stories about contemporary news events are usually called ***news features***. They are more timely, more pressing than personality profiles and colour stories. They have a sense of immediacy, of urgency. The following story about racial conflict in a southern American city is a news feature:

The Uneasy Black-Hispanic Coexistence[1]

By Lynne Duke

Washington Post Service

1 HOUSTON — A black woman, Rose Hawkins, 62, a school cook, has lived among Hispanics for years, and all has been well. But she ticks off the homes where new Hispanics now reside — one next door, another across the street, two down the block, side by side.

2 "They all done moved in," she said.

3 A Hispanic woman, Maria Sanchez, 38, a security guard, arrived in the United States a year ago from Mexico and says that, at first, she was wary of blacks.

4 "When I came, people who were already here would tell me, 'Oh no, there's a black.' You know, 'Close the door,'" said Ms Sanchez, who lives next door to Ms Hawkins.

5 Now, she feels her early caution was unfounded.

6 "Any time my car breaks down," she said, "it's never a Mexican or a white who stops to help me, it's always a black. He may be a pimp or whatever...."

7 She didn't finish, only shrugged.

8 A black woman, LaShay Livingston, 25, a graduate student, gets irritated in the supermarket when she encounters large Hispanic families walking through the aisles.

9 "I just don't understand why everybody has to go," she said.

10 A Hispanic man, Daniel Urquita, 38, who finds work through a street-corner labour pool, said he and others did not want blacks there.

11 "There's another labour pool over at Hardy and Elysian," he said, "but it's too many black people over there. This is

[1] *International Herald Tribune*, Hong Kong, Wednesday, 14 August 1991, No. 33,735, p. 1.

different territory. Black people over there, and Spanish people here."

12 These are the voices of an uneasy coexistence.

13 At a time when the city's Hispanic population is surging so fast it now equals the black population, there is trust between blacks and Hispanics, but also deep suspicion. There is integration, but also basic racism. There is political accommodation, and yet fierce group rivalry....

The lead in this story is is a suspended interest lead because the writer places the reader in the middle of the interview. "Ticks off" is an idiom that makes the overall tone of the piece informal.

In ***Paragraph 2***, notice the colloquial tone of the subject. This provides colour and reinforces the overall informal tone of the piece.

Paragraphs 2, 4, 6, 9, and ***11*** are all full, direct quotes. Notice that the quotes are separate paragraphs. Full, direct quotes make the reader feel close to the people in the story.

Paragraph 12 is a transition from the specific to the general. Beginning with this paragraph, the issue is developed in broader perspective.

A news feature often accompanies a routine news story written as an inverted pyramid. When it does, it is designed to supplement the main story, or act as a ***sidebar*** (see Chapter 1 for more about sidebars).

Colour stories

Some features stories have the sole purpose of creating "atmosphere" for the reader. ***Colour stories***, as they are known, rely heavily on sensory detail — sights, sounds, smells, and so on. Some editors call them ***atmosphere pieces***.

Colour stories often read like fiction. The following excerpt is from a piece describing the effect of an economic recession on an English beach resort city:[2]

[2] *International Herald Tribune*, Hong Kong, Friday, 14 August 1992, No. 34,045, p. 14.

1 BLACKPOOL, England — The harsh wind off the Irish Sea scattered beachgoers along the shore like clumps of seaweed thrown up by the tide. Hats pressed to their temples and windbreakers zipped to their necks, the beachgoers squatted low on the damp sand and stared at the snarling sea.

2 In this way they passed another midsummer's afternoon on the northern England coast.

3 "It's a Blackpool day, it is," Shirley Wright of West Yorkshire said as she hunkered down beside the stone seawall that separates the foaming surf from Blackpool's noisy midway of souvenir shops, tourist arcades and amusement rides. She had been here before and said she was used to the weather by now

4 The winds and thick overcast made the air feel like 50 degrees Fahrenheit, even though the temperature was in the cool-enough mid-60s. August or not, sweaters and jackets are needed....

5 With three steel piers jutting out into the surf, along a seascape dominated by the 101-year-old Blackpool Tower, Blackpool has been the traditional vacation getaway for the armies of factory hands of England's industrial north for more than a century.

6 Many of those factories are gone now, but Blackpool still draws an estimated 9 million to 10 million people a year, including visitors to trade shows and political conventions.

7 For most visitors, the main attractions used to be the sea. Now it's Blackpool's wide variety of oceanfront entertainments, from aquariums and discotheques to pleasure Beach, an amusement park that includes the world's largest collection of wood-stanchioned roller coasters....

This story begins with a ***narrative lead***, which is defined below. Notice the strong visual images and sensory information — "the *harsh* wind", "like *clumps of seaweed thrown up by the tide*", "she *hunkered down beside the stone seawall*", "the *armies* of factory hands".

Here is some colour from a feature story on mortuaries:

> The morgue has an odd smell from the caustic cleaner used to remove any flesh and fibre left on the litters or on the linoleum

> floor. The walls of the large main morgue are white tile bricks, shiny from just having been cleaned. Joseph Flannagan, tour guide and mortuary assistant supervisor, said that a commercial cleaning company had just steam-cleaned the morgue. He thought the cleaner smelled like bubble gum.

Colour may appear in a hard news story. In revising a straightforward news story, an editor might say to a reporter, "Put a little colour in it" — meaning, add some descriptive matter.

Although colour is an end in itself in colour stories, colour may play an important role in other kinds of features, such as personality profiles. For an example of this, see the story *taki* in Chapter 8.

How-To and Where-To Stories

Stories that explain to readers how to do something are known as ***how-to stories***. They can be about anything you can imagine — how to breast feed your baby, how to stay physically fit, how to fix a leaky faucet in your residence.

A similar kind of story is what I call the ***where-to story***. This is a story that tells the consumer where to shop — or what to buy. As an example of this, I will draw upon the work of one of my students in Los Angeles. The student wanted to write a story about the best place to buy chocolate chip cookies. So she listed a series of attributes of cookies that she could measure — price, amount of chocolate chips, texture, freshness, chocolate flavour, and so on — and she created numerical scales to measure them with. Then she invited six friends to accompany her on a trip to several cookie shops in Los Angeles and asked each friend to rate each cookie on each attribute. The final version of the story included a table that summarized the "panel's" findings.

Some journalists refer to stories such as this as ***consumer service articles***, because they provide a service to consumers.

In any case, the journalist should not base the story on his or her own personal experiences, but on some other person's experiences; otherwise, the story does not seem objective.

Featurized Leads

When writing an inverted pyramid story about a spot news event, you don't have much choice about the lead — you are obligated to write the Five W's. This is not true with feature stories, however. In a feature story, a summary lead would be inappropriate. You must find something other than the Five W's for an *opener*, as some writers would say.

When trying to find a way to start a feature story, journalists sometimes say they are *looking for a way to get into the story*. Some say they are *looking for an angle* or *looking for something to hang it on*. Because journalists use several metaphors using the word "hang", they use the word "peg" as well: *What's the peg?* an editor might ask, or: *How are you going to peg that story?*

People who analyze news writing have identified a few common types of feature leads that are effective openers. They include topic leads, twists on clichés, metaphor leads, suspended interest leads, chronological leads, anecdotal leads, and narrative leads. These will be taken up next.

Topic Leads

The topic lead is probably the most basic kind of feature lead. It merely identifies the issue that the news story is about. The next paragraph is a topic lead. It is from a story that reviews an American congressional investigation into organized crime with roots in China and Hong Kong:

> Explosive new evidence about Chinese organized crime reveals how the United States authorities are fighting an uphill battle against the triad invasion from Hong Kong.

The next lead is another topic lead. It is from a story about concerns in the United Kingdom about joining the European Community:

> As Europe braces itself for the crucial Maastricht summit, Britons are beginning to doubt the wisdom of closer unity.

Topic leads are highly functional, but they also are somewhat pedestrian, especially for a colour piece or a personality profile.

Twisting Clichés

This is my favourite kind of feature lead. A twist on a cliché usually is very clever and humorous, however, so it can be done only on a story that is somewhat lighthearted. In that sense, it has only limited applications.

Here is an example:

> MALIBU — Stricter law enforcement has scared the pants back on nude sunbathers here.

The cliché that was "twisted" here is *scared the pants off*, which is a common way that English speakers describe fright: When Americans say something scared their pants off, they are implying that they were so scared, they jumped out of their trousers. Someone who is nude can't jump out of his trousers when he sees a police officer — but he can certainly jump back into them!

Another example makes fun of clichés themselves:

> LOS ANGELES — Clichés about Southern California run about a dime a dozen.

A *dime* is 10 cents, so something that costs *about a dime a dozen* is very cheap — and plentiful. In this lead, the implication is that clichés about Southern California are commonplace.

Clichés are not the only things you can "twist". You can also twist a worn-out or hackneyed image. People always think of sea captains as "going down with their ships" when sinking. Here's a lead from a story about an old man who lived in a decrepit, old hotel and who refused to move when the hotel was being demolished:

> PORTLAND, Ore. — If hotels were ships, John Edwards would go down with one.

Metaphor Leads

Metaphors and similes are closely related. A ***metaphor*** is a statement about a likeness between two things that are ordinarily dissimilar. Example: The Parliament's debate turned into a shooting match between politicians on opposite sides of the aisle.

Sometimes a metaphor can work as a lead:

> SAN FRANCISCO — Imagine a thirsty man bending down at the edge of a vast lake to take a drink of water. Unfortunately, he can take his drink only in the most agonizing fashion, through the thinnest of straws.
>
> This is the problem facing personal computer users who attempt to connect to the profusion of networks, on-line data bases, bulletin boards and electronic mail systems that have sprung up in recent years.

A simile is somewhat like a metaphor. A ***simile*** is a statement using "like" or "as" to draw a comparison between two things. Example: In class, she dressed so well that she looked like a diplomat rather than a student.

As feature leads, similes are weaker than metaphors; however, they are not weak in the body of a story — unless, of course, the comparison that is being drawn is inherently weak in the first place.

Suspended Interest Leads

Suspended interest leads are powerful and effective, but difficult to execute. The ***suspended interest lead*** arouses the interest of the reader and abruptly suspends it, forcing the reader to continue reading the story in order to resolve his heightened interest. Some people call the suspended interest lead a ***grabber***.

Here is one example:

> LONDON — When Mrs. Janet Wynn opened her diary Monday morning, she found the following entry in another person's hand:
>
> "House burgled, 5 a.m."

The lead implies that while Mrs. Wynn slept, someone broke into her residence, stole some items and wrote an entry in her diary as a joke.

One more example:

> TOKYO — When 43-year-old Mayishi Nakagawa woke at 1:45 a.m. Monday, she had no idea that her apartment building was in flames only one thin wall away.

> She heard someone yelling downstairs, but the nuisance of late noise in the building was not unusual. She turned over with annoyance and pulled the covers up to her neck.
>
> That was when she smelled the smoke....

There is another example of a suspended interest lead in Chapter 8, in the story called *taki*. Being able to write such leads obviously depends to some extent on the situations. Police stories are obviously good candidates for such leads.

Chronological Leads

A ***chronological lead*** begins with a time of day, and it usually signals the beginning of a chronological story:

> HONG KONG — It's 9:15 p.m. Jim McKnight, 23, waits quietly in the jockeys' locker room at Happy Valley Racecourse for the sixth race. The 5-foot 4-inch, 110-pound professional already has had a fair evening.
>
> 9:25 p.m. McKnight moves across the locker room to have his weight certified by the clerk of scales, Orene Hampton....

In this story, every paragraph began with a specific time to the nearest minute. This is what I referred to earlier as ***hard chronology***. For more on this, see Chapter 3. I call a similar structure without the specific times a ***soft chronology***.

For example, the last lead could have been written like this:

> HONG KONG — It was late in the evening as Jim McKnight, 23, waited quietly in the jockeys' locker room at Happy Valley Racecourse for the sixth race. The 5-foot 4-inch, 110-pound professional already had had a fair evening.
>
> Moments later McKnight moved across the locker room to have his weight certified by the clerk of scales, Orene Hampton....

Without the specific times, the reader does not know precisely how many minutes passed between each event.

In any case, the hard chronology is perfectly suited for writing a complex crime story. This is because the exact times of events are required to make sense of the way they unfolded, and police records usually include the times of events.

Anecdotal Leads

In Chapter 3, I strongly recommended that you not lead with either a direct quotation or a question. This is true in almost all cases; however, once in a rare while you might see a direct quotation or a question in a lead. Here's one that has both:

> CHICAGO — "Want to make a small fortune trading commodities? Start with a big one."
>
> That old joke frequently makes the rounds at Chicago's commodity exchanges, but many people still haven't heard it, or at least haven't heeded it.[3]

It appears that the lead is a question, but it really is not: The lead is a joke, and the joke has a question in it. The quotes are included to make the joke stand out. *Anecdotes* are little stories that illustrate a point, and jokes are a type of anecdote. This lead in fact is an anecdotal lead, albeit a special type of one. Another special kind of anecdotal lead is the suspended interest lead, which was defined a few pages back.

Leads with questions are extremely weak, and as a result, they are quite uncommon. Whenever a question — or a direct quotation, for that matter — is the best way to lead a story, it will be perfectly obvious to you. Without this kind of certainty, you should avoid them as leads, however.

Narrative Leads

A ***narrative*** is *a story or an account of events.* Most stories begin with a setting, and a narrative lead provides this. In other words, narrative leads establish a setting. Thus the narrative lead opens a news story in the same way that most novels or short stories open:

---

[3] *The Asian Wall Street Journal*, Tuesday, 3 September 1991, Vol. 16, No. 2, p. 1.

> TAIPEI — It rained here Monday night — great gushes of warm rain carried inland by a mild northeasterly monsoon. Tuesday dawned humid and hazy.
>
> Mr. Law Man Fun kicked over his motorscooter and headed into the dense morning commuter traffic. He was only one of tens of thousands of commuters who rely on scooters even though they can afford cars.

There are more examples of narrative leads in the story from Blackpool, earlier in this chapter, as well as in *anna's dream*, Chapter 8, and in *mr. love*, Chapter 9.

Literary Devices and Other Tricks

Now that you've started the feature story, you may find it difficult to continue. The feature is not like the inverted pyramid, which usually presents information in descending order of importance.

For feature stories about people, ***metaphors*** and ***analogies*** can be used to create the image desired. Here is Rex Reed, one of America's most esteemed writers, describing a famous American playwright:

> If a swamp alligator could talk, he would sound like Tennessee Williams. His tongue seems coated with rum and molasses as it darts in and out of his mouth, licking at his moustache like a pink lizard. His voice wavers unsteadily like old gray cigar smoke in a room with no ventilation, rising to a mad cackle like a wounded macaw, settling finally in a cross somewhere between Tallulah Bankhead and Everett Dirksen. His hands flutter like dying birds in an abandoned aviary....[4]

An ***extended metaphor*** can have a powerful effect. Here is an example from Susan Sontag:

> Great writers are either husbands or lovers. Some writers supply the solid virtues of a husband: reliability, intelligibility,

---

[4] From William Ruehlmann, *Stalking the Feature Story* (Cincinnati, Ohio: Writer's Digest, 1977).

> generosity, decency. There are other writers in whom one prizes the gifts of a lover, gifts of temperament rather than of moral goodness. Notoriously, women tolerate qualities in a lover — moodiness, selfishness, unreliability, brutality — that they would never countenance in a husband, in return for excitement, an infusion of intense feeling. In the same way, readers put up with unintelligibility, obsessiveness, painful truths, lies, bad grammar — if, in compensation, the writer allows them to savor rare emotions and dangerous sensations.[5]

An ***analogy*** is a comparison between things that have similar parts or functions. Example: A girl climbs on a horse for the first time, and the horse tries to knock her off its back by running under low branches of trees. The next time she has an opportunity to ride a horse, she refuses, reasoning that all horses will try to knock her off by running under low branches of trees. This is an example of inductive logic using an analogy. As a literary device, it shows up in the newspaper in news analyses and editorials.

Another literary device is irony. The feeling of ***irony*** is one of contradictory and unanticipated emotions created with a sense of detachment. The following illustrates this. It is the end of a story about two hunters who wounded a deer with a bullet. They followed the deer until it could run no longer. They then clubbed it to death with a rifle, but one of the hunters was killed in the process. Following are the last three grafs of the story:

> The buck lifted its head and saw the men. With a lowing grunt and a crippled snap of the neck, it attempted to wedge its front legs beneath its body. The men sprinted across the clearing. Harrington raised his Marlin 30-30 carbine and clubbed the animal down.
>
> The blow splintered the gunstock and the rifle fired. The shot passed over Harrington's shoulder, struck Brown in the chest, and showered out of his back. Alvin Brown, 28, of Readville, Mo., was dead on arrival at the Callaway County Hopsital.
>
> That afternoon, they brought in his deer.[6]

---

[5] Susan Sontag, *Against Interpretation* (New York: Dell Publishing Co. Inc., 1966).

[6] William Ruehlmann, *Stalking the Feature Story* (Cincinnati, Ohio: Writer's Digest, 1977).

This type of ending is sometimes called a ***snapper*** or ***kicker*** because it *snaps* or *kicks* at the reader. The ending reverberates backward through the story, giving it a powerful, retroactive meaning. Such an ending provides excellent ***clozure***, or completion.

This story also illustrates ***tragedy***, which is a common literary device. Unfortunately, much of the news involves human tragedy, so there is no shortage of material for journalists in this regard.

Here is another example of clozure with a snapper. This example is the end of a feature story on what it is like to be a policeman on night duty. Notice the analogy in the first sentence:

> The shift pays itself out slowly like anchor line until the radio crackles with a call about trouble on Fisk Street.
>
> "That's where that woman got cut last night," says Lt. Al Meyer, and heads across town at speed.
>
> Sgt. Don Plageman is already at the scene when Meyer arrives. A heavy-set man in a tee shirt is standing on the sidewalk with a gun in one hand and a blackjack in the other.
>
> "He smashed in the back window of my car," the heavy man raves. "This is the third time."
>
> Plageman tells him to put the weapons away.
>
> A boy who saw someone running from the car offers his assistance.
>
> "You can't miss him," he says. "He's tall."

This illustrates how ***humour*** can be used effectively in the news. The snapper is not only humorous, but also ironic. Its effectiveness is due in part to the fact that it vastly understates the problems that police have in locating criminal suspects. In other words, ***understatement*** can be another powerful device used in the news.

Now that you have seen some of the techniques that characterize feature writing for what it is, it is time to write one. The easiest type of feature probably is the personality profile, which is the subject of the next chapter.

8

Personality Profiles

In this and subsequent chapters, I shall attempt to teach journalistic techniques by means of examples. Here we will examine two personality profiles — *taki* and *anna's dream*.

A ***personality profile*** is a verbal picture of a human being. It's a written portrait. Sometimes it is called merely a ***profile***. The person in the profile is referred to as ***the subject***.

Now, human beings are the most complex organisms on earth. They are multidimensional and *multifaceted* — that is, they have many sides — and successful profiles will introduce the reader to some of these sides. This is worth emphasizing, because personality profiles that fail are usually ones that do not bring out the many sides of the subject's personality.

In other words, unsuccessful profiles typically are *unidimensional.* That is, the reader sees only one side of the subject — and usually the side that the reader sees is the professional, competent one, the career side. Such profiles — and there are many of them, unfortunately — are little more than résumés of the professional careers of their subjects, and they do not challenge the capabilities of the journalist.

Successful profiles, on the other hand, require ingenuity and resourcefulness on the part of the journalist. Assuming that a suitable subject has been selected, there are three basic challenges:

- First, the journalist must identify the subject's most interesting sides, the most interesting aspects of his personality. This may be done through interviews with acquaintances discussed later in this chapter.
- Second, the journalist must tease these out during the interview, getting the subject spontaneously to express these sides of his personality.

Here, proxemics and proper interviewing techniques may make a significant difference. These are discussed in Chapter 6.

• Third, the journalist must capture the results in a news feature, and the news feature, by its nature, is the most difficult form of journalistic writing. Suggestions for writing feature stories are discussed in Chapter 7.

Identifying Subjects for Profiles

There is no community without potential subjects for profiles. There are interesting people everywhere. Although it is natural for the names of prominent and successful people to come to mind when journalists are looking for profile subjects, the field is limitless. Children, the aged, the infirm … , even retarded people may be profile subjects.

The question is not so much one of identifying fascinating people, but one of assessing the interests of the audience and matching these to those of the subject of the profile. Some of these are narrow: For the newspaper audience in Tonga, the life and times of a Tonga graduate student at Beijing University could make a solid, entertaining reading. Other interests are universal: In Sierra Leone, an account of the last days of a young mother dying of AIDS could move readers worldwide to tears.

Researching the Subject

Researching the subject can be as simple or as complex as the journalist wants to make it. Successful, professional subjects are among the easiest to research. They have a body of work. They have a circle of acquaintances. A film director will have films; an author will have books; a corporate executive will have a series of posts he has held in other firms. The more prominent a person is, the more this will be true — and these external, or objective, attributes of a person's career will be available for inspection by the journalist, to some degree.

There are several avenues to explore during the research phase: résumés, newspaper clippings, the subject's works, bibliographic references, and interviews with the subject's acquaintances.

Ask your subject for a résumé. Prominent people keep up-to-date ***résumés*** on file for such purposes, and they are accustomed to this kind of request. They might refer to the résumé as a *C.V.*, an abbreviation for *curriculum vitae*, a Latin phrase that means the same thing.

For people who have already been in the news, you should go to your newspaper's morgue, or library, and see if there are ***newspaper clippings*** on file. If there are none, you may ask the subject himself if he has any clippings of articles about himself. If so, ask for copies. This will help you to avoid going over ground that has been covered before.

If the résumé indicates that books, articles or films have been produced, then attempt to see the ***subject's works***. This is very basic research, and it will head off potential embarrassment: There are few experiences more humiliating for a journalist than to have to ask a famous person what the names of his books or films have been — and what they were about.

Libraries contain ***bibliographic references*** that may contain biographical data on your subject. There are many so-called *Who's Who* books — *Who's Who in America, Who's Who in China, Who's Who in Education, Who's Who in Art, Who's Who in Australia* and so on. There are probably more than 100 such titles in existence. They typically list the date and place of birth, universities attended, marital status, professional positions held, and main works.

Finally, the journalist should not overlook the potential of interviews with the *subject's acquaintances*. By acquaintances, I mean more than just friends and colleagues. Consider interviews with secretaries, servants, students, the subject's children and parents, even people who may not know the subject personally, but who are familiar with the subject's work. A person who is critical of the subject — a rival, an estranged wife — may provide more insight than all of the others together, and this will add a new dimension to the subject.

Selecting a Locale for the Interview

The journalist should arrange for the interview to be conducted at one of the subject's *haunts* — that is, a place frequented by the subject. The subject's residence is an obvious first choice. After this, the second most obvious choice is the subject's office. A restaurant, a club, or a gymnasium may be appropriate, depending on the subject's habits.

Within the haunt itself, the subject might have a favourite spot. In American families, for example, many people sit around the kitchen table and gossip, so the kitchen becomes a favourite place to socialize. In other households, the den is favoured. In any case, the subject probably will have a favourite chair. The journalist should ask the subject to sit in his favourite chair. This will make him feel relaxed and comfortable.

Next, the journalist should express interest in the surroundings. Photographs on a desk, paintings on the wall, knicknacks on bureaus — any of these may have special significance to the subject. Asking about them might open up a personal avenue of discussion that will shed light on the subject's personal interests. They will also give confidence to the subject, because he will be on familiar territory when discussing things that are meaningful to him.

Suggestions from a Professional Profile Writer

There are few people who write personality profiles full time for a prestigious publication. They do exist, however, and I interviewed one about 10 years ago when I was preparing a lecture on profile writing.

His name was Philip Taubman, and he was a writer for *Esquire* magazine, a slick American monthly aimed at upper middle class American males. Mr. Taubman's subjects ranked among the most famous people in America, so he sometimes had to make his first approach to the subject through a publicity agent.

If the response was favourable, Mr. Taubman would undertake extensive research and create an interview schedule. He would then ask to spend about a week with the subject. Ideally, he would live in the subject's residence during the interview phase — eating all meals with the subject, going to the subject's office in the morning, socializing with the subject's acquaintances and accompanying the subject everywhere he went.

Mr. Taubman said that after about three days of intense exposure to the subject, he would return to *Esquire*'s offices in New York and begin writing. At this early freewriting stage, he would identify additional questions that needed to be asked, additional avenues that needed exploration. He would return to visit his subject for at least one more day, this time accompanied by a staff photographer. Mr. Taubman would then interview the subject during the photo session in order to keep the situation naturalistic.

Then he would return to New York and finish the article.

It is unrealistic for most journalists to expect to have this much time to write a personality profile; however, Mr. Taubman's experiences provide a benchmark for the ultimate effort that can be made in this regard.

In the following examples, you will see one in which extensive research was obviously done before an interview — this was for a television profile of American publisher Jann Wenner — and two for which no preparation was done.

Questions from a Live Interview

In this section, I present a list of actual questions asked in an interview with rebel American publisher Jann Wenner. Mr. Wenner is the controversial publisher of *Rolling Stone* magazine. The interview was conducted by Ms Beverly Schuck, a reporter for CNN (Cable News Network). The interview took place in late 1992 on the patio at Wenner's residence in northern California. The complete list of questions appears in Table 8.1.

If you read her questions thoughtfully, you will realize that she researched Wenner's businesses before the interview — he publishes more than just the *Rolling Stone*. For example, Question 18 asks if it is true that one of his publications lost US$20 million.

She asks tough, penetrating questions. In Question 7 she asks Mr. Wenner if he used drugs and was sexually promiscuous in the late 1960s, when he started the *Rolling Stone* — and he candidly admitted that he did use drugs, and that he was sexually promiscuous.

Next she specifically asks about his use of cocaine in Question 8. And she asks if his family was eccentric in Question 9. In Question 29, she asks how much of his ego is tied up in his work.

Other questions are probing, open-ended ones that force Mr. Wenner to explore some of his deepest convictions. For example, Question 10 asks him to recall his childhood heros, and Question 12 asks what he wants to pass on to his children. Question 22 asks what the biggest misconception is that other people have about him. This is a difficult question, because it forces him to repeat what others have said about him that may be overly critical or erroneous, and then to respond to their comments.

The televised interview was only 15 minutes, but some of the responses may have been "edited down", or shortened. In any case, she asked the

Table 8.1 Questions from Jann Wenner Interview

1. What do you remember from that time (in 1967) when you started the magazine?
2. What did you know about the magazine business?
3. What was in your head? What was your vision?
4. What do you attribute your success to?
5. Who supported you in this effort?
6. Would you do it again?
7. Those were wild years then. You did your share of sex, drugs, and rock 'n' roll?
8. How did you keep from becoming addicted to cocaine?
9. I read that your family was affluent but eccentric. Would you describe them that way?
10. Do you remember having heros as a child?
11. What did you get from each parent?
12. What do you want to pass on to your children?
13. What do you know about the secret to a long and happy marriage?
14. What do you and your wife do together?
15. What has been the single biggest impact your children had on your lifestyle?
16. How much are you willing to risk on "Men's Journal" magazine?
17. You have a two-year commitment?
18. "Us" magazine lost $20 million?
19. When will it break even?
20. When does it make a profit?
21. How have your ideas of success changed in 25 years?
22. What is the biggest misconception about you?
23. What is the thing you want people to understand about you?
24. For 25 years ... you haven't had to do anything you didn't want to ... ?
25. What do you like the best about your job?
26. Will you write some day?
27. There's no book in you?
28. If not this career, what?
29. How much of your ego is tied up in this?

questions in a very short time span. When you plan your interview questions for a profile, use these as a guide.

taki

The following story is a personality profile that breaks some of the rules I gave previously, but it is cleverly done. From the context, it appears that the writer did not have much time to spend with the subject. The subject met the writer in the lobby of a hotel, and the interview was conducted over luncheon. In reading the story, see if you can tell what the questions were, and notice how the writer handled the responses. The story is discussed more fully in the next section of this chapter.

High Life, Women and Jail: Taki Talks[1]

By Martha Sherrill
Washington Post Service

1 WASHINGTON — A young woman called, a publicist: "Taki thought you might want to know what he looks like."

2 But his photograph is on the book jacket.

3 "That won't help, I'm afraid."

4 What will?

5 "He'll be wearing a blue blazer," she said, then broke into a giggle. "And he's very tan." Gold pinkie ring, macho sport watch, tan infinitum.... Taki wiped some sweat in the Hay-Adams lobby. A five-block dash in the heat had temporarily impaired the power of his charm.

6 Once he had cooled off, his personality returned. It is dry, bottomless, British. It is nearly impossible to resist, like stepping into quicksand in the Sahara. He offered naughty quips and wickedness, sly compliments and flirtations. He's a rake. You could tell by the way he threw his blue blazer over one shoulder. He's a rogue. You could tell by his gruesome, baritone, rich-guy, haunted-house laugh. Soon the afternoon

---

[1] *International Herald Tribune*, Hong Kong, Saturday–Sunday, 31 August–1 September 1991, No. 33,750, p. 20.

talk turned to scandals, commies and the Kennedys. Liberals were bashed. The media did not survive. Nothing repeatable.

7 Talky Taki! Tacky Taki!

8 A gossip columnist for the Spectator in London — his byline is simply Taki — he wears his good manners without a hint of stuffiness or the slightest prison smell. He is Greek. He is rich. He is conservative. And he is assured … by his blazer, his tan, his ring, his address book, his father's yacht, his years at boarding school, his days at the University of Virginia.

9 Who cares that's he's a felon?

10 "I lost some Greek shipowner friends," Taki said, when asked if his three-month stay in a British jail for cocaine possession in 1985 had damaged him socially. "Very respectable — the middle class. They were shocked, shocked! Alas, thank God, I didn't lost a single upper-class friend, which sounds awful. I certainly didn't lose any working class friends."

11 Names of stalwart friends, although certainly not any working-class ones, were mentioned with some frequency. Bill Buckley. Jay McInerney. More assurances. Lobbed like little tennis balls, their names bounced across the luncheon table. Gianni Agnelli. Thunk-thunk-thunk!

12 "The International Jet Set" may seem like a hoary term from the '70s — wind-free yachts and oily tans and George Hamilton suavely pushing his way into black-and-white photographs with Jackie and Ari — but Taki still keeps score in that dead universe.

13 Until Taki was 30, he was just a rich Greek smoothie. He played tennis. He skied. He got a black belt in karate. He waited for the family money — the Theodoracopulos shipping and textile fortune — to cruise closer his way. And he chased women.

14 His social ties would come to help him professionally. In 1968 he impressed a Newsweek correspondent named Arnaud de Borchgrave — a Belgian count, don't you know? — by effortlessly introducing him to Gianni Agnelli, and in turn de Borchgrave encouraged Taki to become a paparazzo for

Newsweek. After two years of this "fun" and "horrendous" work, he became a correspondent for an Athenian daily.

15 Fourteen years ago, he started writing a society column called "High Life" for the Spectator. He was never dull. Countless gossipy missives for Vanity Fair, then Connoisseur and National Review, ensued.

16 Of his days before deadlines, he said, "I had no job. I just played tennis. You always have a raison d'etre to pick up girls."

17 Women. It takes about two minutes with Taki to realize that "blindly chasing pretty girls" — as he so aptly puts it — has been his true life's work. He admits this with relish and zest, despite his second marriage in 1981 to Alexandra Schoenburg-Hartenstein, an Austrian princess. And despite their two children, 15 and 11, born out of wedlock.

18 In his newly released jail memoirs, "Nothing to Declare," Taki, 52, describes himself as "obsessed with women" and "always in love."

19 He has described himself as "proud to be a male chauvinist."

20 "At least in the society where I grew up," Taki goes on, "we honor and respect women, we protect and provide for them," and, of course, he added, deceive them at will.

21 In his politically incorrect Spectator column, he often talks of "girls" and "cutie pies." They never seem to have names, or the kind he cares to drop.

22 In "Nothing to Declare," he tells the story of how he wound up in Pentonville prison, one of the oldest in Britain, for three months. Going through customs at Heathrow, he was discovered carrying an envelope containing 20 grams of cocaine. After a trial, he was sentenced.

23 On the eve of his incarceration, the Spectator threw him a wild bash. Ha. Ha. John Aspinall ("England's greatest gambler and poshest party-giver," writes Taki) threw him another.

24 His children were sent off to New York, after being told Daddy was going to Australia to do research for a book.

25 His cell was 13 feet by 7 feet. He slept with two dirty blankets. He worked as a gym orderly. He told everybody who asked that, on the outside, he was a waiter in a Greek restaurant.

26 He kept a diary. He wrote down the cool language to use. The names to know. His impressions. He became fascinated by the personalities in jail, their lives, their crimes.

27 Did he lay on the responsible-and-possibly-reformed-Taki business a little thick in the book? "Yes. I think so," he said. He did this, he claimed, for his wife and children.

28 "Alexandra's a wonderful girl, I mean, she's a serious woman," he said. "She didn't care — we don't care about these things — but for the children, it's awful. They will always have a father who went to jail."

29 He lives in London, New York and Athens. He has places too, "inherited family houses," in Southampton and Switzerland and elsewhere. His father died in 1989, leaving a business worth £100 million (about $168 million), according to the London Daily Telegraph, but Taki won't discuss his inheritance for tax reasons.

30 "I just say," he said, "that everything belongs to Mother."

31 Is he a traitor to his class, by being a journalist, by writing about the rich?

32 "What class?" he asked rhetorically, shaking his head. "The class betrayed itself when it traded manners for money. The class betrayed itself long before I betrayed it. They sold their good houses and put up apartment buildings. They got rid of their old wives for new models. The class isn't what it used to be."

33 Last month, Sylvester Stallone successfully sued him for libel — after Taki had accused Rambo of "ducking the Vietnam War" in a February Spectator column. When Stallone protested, Taki dared him into court. The columnist and his magazine agreed to pay an undisclosed amount in damages and legal costs.

34 Taki has been a conservative since the Communists tried to take over Greece. "They killed all my father's factory workers, but they didn't get us," he said.

35 He described his father as "once the greatest womanizer in Greece."

36 Women are a topic that he can't keep himself from addressing, no matter how the anecdote begins:

37 "When they lowered Father into the family crypt, it was a hot day — just like this," he said. "The prime minister was there, helping my mother.... And this girl came in — very young — and threw a flower, just as the thing went in. So afterward, I saw her. And I thought, 'Oh, I can't pick up a girl at my father's funeral.' But I was very close to it.

38 "I said to her, 'I saw what you did. It was a very noble, touching gesture. Who are you?'

"She said, 'You know who I am.'"

39 His father's girlfriend, of course.

40 "Another 19-year-old!"

41 How about you, Taki?

42 "The girl I'm currently romancing? She's 26."

43 Seems respectable enough.

44 "Yes," he replied, "but she's married."

Annotations to *taki*

This story illustrates the power of short, punchy sentences. The *taki* story has 1,335 words and 124 sentences, making an average sentence length of 10.8 words. Note that there is a 1-word sentence in ***Paragraph 17***. There are five 1-word sentences in this story. And if you look carefully, you will see there are ten 2-word sentences and six 3-word sentences.

This story also illustrates the effectiveness of portraying the many sides of a personality. On the one hand, we see Taki as a handsome, polished and sophisticated man, someone who, because of his success as a columnist, might even be considered an *artiste*. On the other hand, we see him also as a liar, an adulterer, and a hypocrite.

Paragraph 1 is a *suspended interest lead*. This kind of lead is defined and illustrated in Chapter 7. In this story the writer places the reader in the middle of a developing situation by means of an intriguing quote. Notice that the attribution is done with a colon. This technique is illustrated on Page 86; it is grammatically correct, but the technique is easily overworked, so don't use it excessively.

In ***Paragraphs 2*** and ***4***, notice how the journalist "talks" to the publicist. She does this without using quotation marks and without using the first person.

In ***Paragraph 6*** the second sentence contains a simple series, but "and" is omitted — *dry, bottomless, British*. This makes the series succinct, possibly reflecting the personality of the subject. Later in this paragraph, extensive use of colour creates a compelling image of the subject — *... he threw his blue blazer over one shoulder ... , his gruesome, baritone, rich-guy, haunted-house laugh*. The writer feeds this information to the reader with strong, parallel structures — *You could tell by.... You could tell by....*

In ***Paragraph 8***, we find another series of strong parallel sentences — *He is Greek. He is rich. And he is assured....* This series of short sentences has a powerful, punchy, staccato effect, almost as though the writer were a boxer dancing around the subject, jabbing at him with her fists. Another series of short, parallel sentences appears in ***Paragraph 13***.

Paragraph 9 is an example of a teaser. A ***teaser*** is a paragraph that *teases* the reader: It tempts the reader to continue by providing some curious information. What could *he's a felon* possibly mean? The only way to answer this is to read on.

In ***Paragraph 11***, *thunk-thunk-thunk* is the sound of the *little tennis balls* being lobbed, figuratively speaking, onto the table while they are eating lunch. Using words like these is called ***onomatopoeia***, or the use of words designed to imitate sounds.

In ***Paragraph 20***, the subject's hypocrisy is clearly laid out for the reader to see. The writer is setting up Taki for a series of harsh blows. In ***Paragraphs 24***, ***26***, and ***27*** we see that he lies to his children; he lies to other inmates in prison; he lies in his book about being reformed and responsible.

Paragraph 23 contains an interesting segment — *Ha. Ha.* Normally in English when we want to indicate that someone is laughing spontaneously, we write *Ha-ha!* On the other hand, when people want to suggest laughter sarcastically, they say *Ha. Ha.* in a very controlled, unemotional way. In other words, the writer here is indicating that she doesn't think Taki's comments are very funny — although *he* apparently does.

Paragraph 27 contains an interesting syntactical construction — *the responsible-and-possibly-reformed-Taki business*. The hyphenated expression is a compound adjective that modifies the word "business".

anna's dream

The next example is from Hong Kong. It is a story about a prostitute, and it was written by one of my students. The student initially proposed to write a story about prostitution because recent police statistics indicated a rise in the number of foreign prostitutes in the region. However, other media had already covered much of the story.

I suggested that, rather than following other media's dry statistical accounts, the writer should take a more personal approach, perhaps telling the story of a single prostitute. The following resulted:

Anna's Dream: A prostitute in Sham Shui Po tells her story[2]

By Clarence Tsui

1 A young, carefully turned out woman stands every evening in the same dark doorway on a back street in Sham Shui Po. Seedy villas stretch along the broken pavement, and bright neon signs hang crookedly from the buildings, blazing in the cold night.

2 The young woman shifts on her feet and patiently waits.

3 She is not standing there for fun. She is working — or, more precisely, waiting for work to come her way.

4 "I work here because this job pays, and it pays much more than my previous ones, such as busing dishes in a restaurant. Money is the main factor," says Anna.

5 Anna, who declines to reveal her real name, is 23. She is one of several women who wait in doorways along Fuk Wa and Kwai Lin Streets in Sham Shui Po as dusk approaches. She wears heavy make-up and a black dress with lace. Loud

[2] *Varsity* magazine, The Chinese University of Hong Kong, February 1994, pp. 9–10.

earrings betray her profession, which goes by different names, ranging from the elegant-sounding "escort", to the Cantonese street slang "chicken", and to the official word "prostitute".

6 The problem of prostitution in Hong Kong has existed for decades. Having exerted much effort to wipe out underage prostitutes in Mong Kok, the government now faces a new headache — foreign prostitutes in Sham Shui Po.

7 Anna, originally from Thailand, is one of them. Unfortunately, her situation is the result of a shattered dream more than anything else.

8 "I came here five years ago, when I was only 18," she explains in fluent Cantonese. "I married a Chinese construction worker and came with him to Hong Kong. I just wanted to get away from the poor life that I led in Thailand, where I worked as a salesgirl in a store.

9 "However, my husband turned out to be very lazy — and, what's more, he gambled a lot. He didn't give me any money, and it was hard (to survive), since, besides supporting myself and my son, I had to look after my parents in Thailand also.

10 "Eventually I left him. But he refused to divorce, fearing that he had to pay me alimony. As a result, I was left really strapped for cash then.

11 "I worked in many Thai restaurants after that. I knew many other Thai women there, and since then I have begun to work here in Sham Shui Po," she says.

12 According to Anna, the job pays well. She receives $200 from each customer, and each one takes only about 15 minutes.

13 She gets about seven to eight customers each night during her four-hour stint from 5 to 9 p.m., she says.

14 "My friends who used to be in this job had earned enough money, and most of them have already gone back to Thailand," she says.

15 Not all of Anna's friends work in the streets, though. Some of them work in nightclubs in Tsim Sha Tsui.

16 She says, "I don't work there because I can't speak English, and it's boring working in a nightclub anyway.

17 Prostitution is not a major political issue in Hong Kong. Although police are concerned about brothels and hotels selling the services of underage girls and drugs, the main focus of discussion about prostitution in Hong Kong concerns venereal diseases. Prostitutes are thought to be fearless — perhaps ignorant — of these ailments, but Anna denies that.

18 "I make sure my customers wear condoms every time. No condom, no business. In contrast to what people say, it is the customers who sometimes insist on not wearing one," she says.

19 "My friends and I are very careful about it. None of the people I know has been infected with AIDS, for example. We'd rather not earn the money than run the risk."

20 About the type of people who give them business, Anna says that they are mostly in their 30s. They are better behaved than most pornographic films or mass media suggest.

21 "Customers never beat or physically abuse me, although I am shouted at occasionally," she says.

22 "The problems with them mostly concern haggling over the amount to be paid — and wearing condoms."

23 Although reports of prostitution often relate it to triad activities, Anna's experience is relatively free of criminal connections.

24 "My friends and I who work here have never been controlled by any triad organizations. We work for ourselves and receive all we are paid," she says.

25 "Occasionally, triad members will come by and ask for protection money, and we duely pay. I've heard of instances in which people were beaten up when they didn't pay the money.

26 "Other than that, we work for ourselves. The triad people do not come often. I haven't seen them for the past few days.

27 "We do this according to our own will — there is nobody who makes us work in such a place."

28 Concerning the police, they cannot arrest Anna without evidence of criminal activity because she holds a Hong Kong identity card. Her relationship with the police is therefore far from a cat-and-mouse one.

29 "Of course, I don't want to be seen by police officers, but they could not take me away for being an illegal immigrant," Anna says.

30 "Sometimes I even get to banter with them when they pass me by. Some of them are surprised by my fluent Cantonese. They say to me, 'Tell us if any triad members try to harass you or squeeze money out of you.'"

31 Since Anna is not being kept as a prisoner by triad members, she is free to go anywhere when she is not working. She says she lives in a flat in Kowloon City with her Thai friends.

32 "They all used to work here, but now most of them have retired from this job. Some of them have even married.

33 "During daytime, when I am not working, I stay at home. I don't do much shopping because money is tight. I buy clothes occasionally because we need to have some flashy clothes in our work," Anna says.

34 When asked about her feelings when she has to have sex with unknown people for money, Anna appears embarrassed.

35 "Well ..., every time I tell myself that it is just for money, it is just another job, and this makes me feel better.

36 "Now, I'm very indifferent to it.

37 "I've got no regrets about taking up this job because it provides me with enough money to support both myself and my family in Thailand, who need money more desperately than I do," she says.

38 Even so, Anna seems, in a sense, ashamed of her profession.

39 "I have told my parents that I am working as a waitress in a restaurant. I don't think that they could bear my being a prostitute," she says.

40 "My husband here does not want to see me, either. I have not seen my son for nearly a year now. I think his father is very ashamed of me and would rather like the child to forget me," she sighs.

41 Talking about her future, Anna says that she would like to stay in Hong Kong.

42 "Once I think I have earned enough, I will change my job to a waitress, a salesgirl or something like that. For the time being — like at least the next year or two — I'll carry on with this job," Anna says.

43 "Maybe after I have quit this job, I'll remarry.... Who knows? One thing for sure — I will never tell him about this part of my story."

Annotations to *anna*

The student who wrote this story at first felt very uncomfortable with the idea of approaching a prostitute for an interview. He was certain that no prostitute would talk to him. And although he did not say this, I suspect he felt very shy about talking to one in the first place.

In any case, the story worked, and a good lesson to learn from his experience is that you can never predict how people will respond to your requests as a journalist. If you at least take the initiative, you may be rewarded with an excellent piece requiring little or no effort.

Turning now to ***Paragraph 1***, note that this is a *narrative lead*: It describes a setting. In doing so, it makes use of *colour* — "seedy villas", "broken pavement", "crooked signs", and so on.

In ***Paragraph 2***, note that the present tense is invoked, and it is used throughout the story in all of the attribution and descriptive matter. As a literary device, this is known as the ***historical present***, and its purpose is *to make past events seem more contemporary, to bring the reader closer to the events*. It is a common technique in feature writing.

In ***Paragraph 6***, however, note that the verb "has existed" is in the present perfect tense. One problem that beginning writers have with the historical present is not knowing when to shift out of it.

In ***Paragraph 5***, note how the writer establishes her identity. Anna "declines to reveal her real name". This is succinct and appropriate. The reader understands why. This paragraph also has some good examples of colour — "black dress with lace", "loud earrings".

Paragraph 6 provides the reader with background to put the story in context.

Paragraphs 39 and ***40*** reveal Anna's shame, thus providing deep poignancy to the story.

Paragraph 43 is a kicker or snapper defined in the last chapter.

In conclusion, it is possible to do a readable personality profile without much preparation, but the more the preparation, the better the story.

9
The Narrative

The narrative style of writing is a relative newcomer to the newspaper business. It has a longer history in books and magazines, however. In recent years in the newspaper business, the narrative style has come into its own, so to speak; that is, it has matured and taken a separate identity, principally through a vehicle known as ***new journalism***. In my view, new journalism is only a new label for a news structure that has existed, in one form or another, for many decades, but that evolved to its most sophisticated form in the 1960s under the bylines of Truman Capote, Rex Reed, Tom Wolfe, Joan Didion, Gay Talese, Jimmy Breslin and Susan Sontag.[1]

A ***narrative*** is an article relating a sequence of events, but it does this in a manner that approaches the style of fiction. The objective, to relate a sequence of events, suggests that the underlying structure should be chronological. Indeed, in most cases, the narrative resembles the soft chronology, which I defined on Page 63 and illustrated with a short article on Pages 61–62. However, the narrative departs from the soft chronology in a number of very significant ways.

For one, it might shift back and forth in time, using ***flashbacks*** or going back in time, as the need arises, to heighten the reader's interest in the narration — to build suspense or to address an unanswered question. In extreme cases, it might even relate events in *reverse chronological order*, in what is known as an ***inverted*** or ***reverse chronology***.

---

[1] For a collection of narrative essays, see Tom Wolfe's *The New Journalism* (New York: Harper and Row, 1973). One of the best book-length treatments is Truman Capote's *In Cold Blood* (New York: Random House, 1966).

For another, the narrative is rich in descriptive detail. Its purpose goes beyond that of the ordinary news story; its purpose is to *tell a story*, to *portray a series of dramatic events*, not merely to present the news. Tom Wolfe, a leading practitioner of the style, referred to it as *saturational*, meaning that the reporter immerses himself in details and tries to reconstruct events for reader. Such details might include the manners, habits and customs of the people in the story; they might include furnishings, automobiles, the weather....

Finally, its format is unique among the structures for reporting news events. Not only is it considerably longer, but it uses longer sentences and longer paragraphs. Some of these paragraphs may even have topic sentences and they may be constructed in a manner similar to that taught in traditional English composition.

mr. love

With this background, we can now turn to an example of this style to see how these ideas are put into practice:

Mr. Love's Secret Life and Public Death[2]

By Cathy Horyn and Patricia Dane Rogers

Washington Post Service

1 WASHINGTON — To begin with, there was the body: black male, 200 pounds, naked on a sleigh bed. He was dead, all right, dead and lying face up on a taupe coverlet with a stone pineapple stuck in his head. There were slashes across his ankles and testicles, but these appeared to have been an afterthought — a case of overkill with a serrated knife. What had killed him was the pineapple, and the fact that it had crushed his skull and remained there for three days was an indication of how deadly a 40-pound finial can be when used as a murder weapon.

2 Something else surprised Detective Ray Crawford that afternoon. Until he walked into the bedroom at 3133 Connecticut

[2] *International Herald Tribune*, Hong Kong, Saturday–Sunday, 13–14 February 1993, p. 20.

Avenue with Sergeant Walter Staples and four other detectives from the District of Columbia police homicide squad, he had assumed the victim was white. It was the address, he said. Moreover, it was an apartment in the Kennedy-Warren, and it seemed to Crawford, who is black, that this was the sort of place where a white person would live: an apartment that did not have a couch but did have a French settee; that did not have a dining room but did have an Empire table set with topiaries and silver-framed pictures. It was the kind of apartment, in other words, that belonged to someone who had understood the surface of things, and it was this impression, more than the actual details, that made Crawford believe the man on the sleigh bed was not entirely who he appeared to be. Nothing about the living room or the library, with its pretty green wallpaper, suggested there had been a struggle, and so the detectives focused their investigation on the bedroom, a room done in shades of beige with khaki swags over the windows that were edged with five-inch bullion fringe. There were certain inconsistencies about the room. For example: The victim's clothes had been placed on a chair, but the closet and the drawers of the dresser appeared to have been opened and gone through. "But neatly," said Crawford. On the evidence of this, and the fact that several watches and articles of clothing were later discovered to be missing, the detectives concluded that robbery had been the motive. And given the condition of the room, its relative neatness in the face of mayhem, the detectives also concluded that the killer had been in the apartment before. "We knew he had been a friend," said Crawford. But what was most interesting about this premise was something that was still in the apartment, something that perhaps the killer had seen as he reached for the stone pineapple. On a high table at the head of the bed was an arrangement of silver frames, not unlike those in the living room, and Crawford looked at them. Here were people who had known the victim — friends, presumably. Women in evening clothes, men in black tie: people, it seemed to Crawford, in high places. More than once that day, and for several days to come, the detective would look at those pictures and the ones arranged amid the topiaries and say to himself, "This was someone who was photographed with the Queen of England and Barbara Bush. Who was this guy? Who was he?"

3 As it turned out, he was Kenneth P. Love, the 42-year-old son of a retired army master sergeant and a cafeteria supervisor, and at 3:25 P.M. on Dec. 21, approximately 60 hours after he had last been seen alive, he was officially pronounced dead by the medical examiner of the District of Columbia. Of course, he had been more than the son of a noncommissioned officer, and that was precisely the point that lifted the details of his death into apologue. He was Kenneth Love, the florist. Kenneth Love, whose clients included Oatsie Charles, Marion Rosenthal, Katharine Graham, Deeda Blair, Jennifer Phillips, Ruthie Leffall, Ann Jordan, Amie Block and Patsy Preston, whose corporate clientele included Red Sage, the Ritz-Carlton, the Phillips Collection and The Washington Post, and whose murder now produced conflicting feelings of grief and doubt.

4 "I've never seen so many big-dealers in this town upset about anything as this," said the Georgetown decorator Anthony P. Browne, who was in Newport with Robert and Oatsie Charles when he heard the news about Love. And indeed, before the body had reached the city morgue, before it had been tagged and positively identified by a member of the family, there was a sense of circuits lighting up along the coast, of phones ringing off the hook.

5 At Templeton, the Long Island estate of C.Z. Guest, there were recollections of conversations going back 15 years. "He would call me for advice about flowers. He would ask about combinations — what went with what and I told him most flowers get along with each other," said the gardening columnist and wife of the late sportsman Winston Guest. "I hadn't heard from him for a long time and asked Oatsie in Newport last summer, 'Where the hell is Kenneth?' He used to call me if anything went wrong. He meant a lot to a lot of us."

6 In Newport, where the Charleses had gone the morning of Dec. 18, leaving two notes with the maid in Georgetown for

Love to deliver with flowers to Deeda Blair and Buffy Cafritz, the grief was palpable. "Anthony Browne is sitting here, and he and Robert and I were talking about it," she said the day after the body was discovered. "I'm not going to feel the same about Washington. What are we going to do without Kenneth?" Her voice dropped. "Who will do our flowers, mend the china or rearrange the furniture? Who will say this chair ought to be moved there? There is no one."

7 On Dec. 26, at 2:30 P.M., a Service of Christian Burial was offered for Kenneth Love at the Church of the Holy Communion on Martin Luther King Avenue in Southeast. Some 100 mourners watched the family walk up the aisle and enter the first pews on the right — parents Ramona and John walking between two grandchildren, brothers Darryl, Eric and Steve holding babies against their shoulders, sister Cindy. They heard the Reverend Frederick Quinn speak of Love's "restless, entrepreneurial side," heard him say that "our Lord was no stranger to violent death." They may or may not have wondered who among them had witnessed that "restless, entrepreneurial side," since there was only one client present — Deeda Blair, who came with her husband, the former ambassador William McCormick Blair — and a handful of close friends, a number owing perhaps to the holidays but more to the fact that until Love died, none of his clients and very few of his friends knew that his parents lived just across the Anacostia River, and that he had grown up in a little white bungalow shaded by green aluminum awnings and surrounded by a cyclone fence.

8 And, as it turned out, they would know more about him dead than alive, for on Jan. 5, 10 days after the funeral, police arrested a 19-year-old man named David Rider and charged him with felony murder in the death of Kenneth Love. According to the detectives, David Rider was a hustler and Love, he told them, had been his sugar daddy.

9 In the spring of 1958, John Love was stationed at Fort Gordon, Georgia, and living with his wife and four small sons in a house on Gregg Street in Augusta. If John Love felt any

personal indignities as a black man living in a state where the Ku Klux Klan was operating openly, he was not the kind of man who expressed those feelings publicly. In any case, he had already begun to instill in his oldest child certain beliefs, among them, he said, "that God made us all." To John Love, and perhaps to his son, "color made no difference at all."

10 In May of 1958, John Love was transferred to West Germany, and in August, Ramona and the children followed for what was supposed to have been a four-year tour. "But Mr. Khrushchev was rattling his sabers in Berlin," he said, "so we stayed another six months." That was 1962. By the spring of 1963, John Love was assigned to the Pentagon, and the family, which now included Cindy, was living in a cramped rental on Atlantic Street. "They put up with that place, and then I thought, 'Why pay rent?'" he recalled. "'Why not buy a little house?'" And so in 1966, John Love took his savings and bought a white bungalow on Brothers Place. The next year he was sent to Vietnam. He would return for another tour in 1972, and remain there through the fall of Saigon.

11 It was clear to anyone who knew Kenneth in those days that he wanted other things for himself. At Ballou High School, where the anthems of the civil rights movement and the black power struggle would eventually be heard, he insisted on wearing a tie, even an ascot, and carrying his books in a briefcase. With a resourcefulness that now seems prescient, he began to cultivate friendships in Georgetown and Tenley, taking the bus across the Anacostia River.

12 By the time he entered George Washington University in the fall of 1968, his wardrobe included not only ties but suits and oxford cloth shirts and loafers, which he began to wear without socks. "He stood out like a foreign student," recalled a classmate. And, in a way, he was. The years abroad had left an impression, and he didn't hesitate to tell people that he had grown up in Germany or, at other times, "all over the world." But whatever four years of base life had shown him, it was not the same as being black in Washington. It was certainly not

the same as being black and gay in Washington, at least not to Kenneth Love.

13 For a while in the mid-'70s he seemed to be everywhere at once. He was in the bar at the Georgetown Inn having drinks. He was at the Watergate arranging table settings for William Miller Gifts, where he worked briefly after college. He was living at the Altamont Apartments on Wyoming, then a house on Corcoran Street. It seemed to a lot of people then that Love, who already knew so much about wine and architecture and the intricacies of serving tea, was destined for greater things.

14 There was, of course, the more mundane problem of earning a living, and in the spring of 1976, without any apparent capital of his own, Love opened a gift shop on Wisconsin Avenue with several backers, among them a radiologist at Georgetown University Hospital named John C. Harbert.

15 Kenneth Love Inc. was an immediate sensation. "I bought there, like a fool," said the decorator Frank Randolph. "We all did." The place was so filled with orchids and Rigaud candles and antique tables set with Limoges and silver flatware that one might have thought it was a private dining room.

16 By April of the following year, Love was ready to expand his circle further, and he telephoned C.Z. Guest in New York.

17 "He called me out of the blue and said he'd like to give a tea for me in Washington," said Guest, who had just published her first gardening book. "He was going to meet me at the plane. I didn't know he was black. So, I get off the plane and I'm looking for him. He had told me he'd be in a red MG. Listen, I was brought up with black servants — the stables and all — and there he was in this red MG. He was so divine. Had lovely manners. The minute I came out he was waving at me, black as coal. I got into at MG with the top down and drove into Washington. I was brought up in Boston with white and black servants, but I never heard a black man speak like a white man before Kenneth.

18 "Guess what we did? I told him I'd like to introduce him to Oatsie Charles, and he drove right over to Oatsie's house.

I'll never forget the look on her black butler's face when he opened the door and saw Mrs. Guest with a black man. I introduced myself and we went into the drawing room. We had the best time.

19 "He knew I knew a lot of people. I can see him now in that red MG, always well dressed. He wasn't an unattractive homosexual. He was the most warm, delightfully charming person. And I have never had such delicious tea sandwiches as at that tea for me."

20 If Guest was revealing of her class, Love had managed to conceal almost everything about his. "I always had the idea his parents were from North Carolina or someplace," said Anthony Browne. To Randolph, he mentioned the existence of American Indian blood in his family, and said his father had been a colonel in the army. Most of his friends knew about a grandmother in Philadelphia, and one day in the '70s Love turned up wearing a gold Cartier watch that he said she had given him. Along with the Brooks Brothers suits and starched collars, he acquired a clipped manner of speaking, and a hyphen between middle and last names. He was Kenneth Phoenix-Love.

21 None of this, of course, seemed particularly calculated or suspect in a country that considers upward mobility an inalienable right. In any case, the degree of self-invention did not compare with the level of deception being practiced on the Small Business Administration, which in the spring of 1978 was preparing to sue the owners of Kenneth Love Inc. to recover $39,400 in a defaulted SBA minority loan. According to an internal memo dated April 13, 1978, from the Vega Investment Corp., which then owned the building on Wisconsin Avenue, the SBA considered Kenneth Love Inc. "a bummer" and had asked the FBI to investigate, among other things, the appropriation of auctionable inventory from the shop. At the same time, Vega placed a lien on the business for unpaid rent for the months of February and March after five letters to Love, who was then living at John Harbert's house in Georgetown, had gone unanswered. "It appeared," according

to a spokesman for Vega, "that he had no intention of paying the rent due."

22 By then, Love had abandoned the shop. And what might have been anyone's routine business failure, anyone's case of bad judgment and debt and overextension, now took on the additional element of acrimony. There were accusations of theft and fraud, of merchandise ordered but unaccountably lost. "A customer would come in to order five place settings of Limoges," said one of the backers, "and Kenneth would take the money but never place the order." (It would come out , in an interview with a previous employer, that Love had been of accused of taking a gold Cartier watch in a similar way, and been dismissed.) It would also become clear to Harbert, when he returned from sabbatical in the spring of 1978, that Love had not only failed to manage the business but had paid neither rent nor taxes. "When John found out what was going on," said an attorney hired by Love to represent him in the landlord's suit, "he gave Kenneth about five minutes to pack his bags." Harbert could not be reached for comment.

23 If Love was culpable, it is also possible that he was made a scapegoat by people legally bound to protect the creditors' interests. In the end they settled the debt. As for Love, he moved on. By 1979 he had taken up landscaping, and was working out of a garage on Capitol Hill owned by an importer of Haitian art named Nathaniel Bunyan Knight.

24 It was around this time that Oatsie Charles met a doctor who said he knew Love. "I believe he was in the radiology department at Georgetown," she recalled. "He told me, 'You wouldn't be so fond of Kenneth if you knew what he was really like.'"

25 "Well," Charles said in retrospect, "I didn't want to know."

26 The new decade did not seem to lend itself to introspection. Between giving and going to parties, decorating and redecorating their homes, and keeping up with the latest political maneuvering, the people who invariably counted as society in Washington in the '80s were kept busy. For Love, it would be an era of extraordinary achievement.

27 Although landscaping had given him something to do after the shop closed, it could not hold his interest nor, apparently, satisfy his ambitions. "I may have been one of the first to use him as a florist," said Jennifer Phillips. "I used Kenneth as soon as [David] Ellsworth was finished."

28 It was perhaps a measure of her disregard for gossip that no client came closer to understanding Love's true nature, his reasons for ambiguity and the potential for self-hatred, than Oatsie Charles. "We used to have extraordinary conversations completely open and not at all what anyone would call 'PC,'" recalled Charles. "I used to say to him, 'C'mon, Kenneth, your grandmother didn't bring you up with these things. Where did you get them?' There was never the slightest feeling of class or race, just two people who knew exactly what they were talking about."

29 Of course, she never put much stock in what the doctor had to say about Love. "I understood," she said. "God knows if I'd come up the way Kenneth did, if I had to fight my way to get to the top table, there's no telling what I would do."

30 Charles paused, as though she weren't quite sure she had come to the heart of the matter, and then she said, more forcefully, "He couldn't be a Vernon Jordan or a Ron Brown. He just plain didn't want to be black."

31 By the spring of 1988, when Love was living in the Kennedy-Warren and moving among a clientele that now wanted his opinion not only on flowers but on furniture and place settings, he had begun to demonstrate a preference for young, white men, men who could often be found at 3 A.M. in an alley and who, for the promise of payment or some other tangible asset, would have sex with him.

32 At such times, and in such places as Badlands and the Fraternity House, he was known as "Mr. Love," in deference perhaps to his clothes — he would often go straight to the bars from a black-tie event at the Phillips Collection or the Kennedy Center — but more to the fact that in choosing men who by their very circumstances were dependent and willing to be used, he had chosen a class of people to whom he could be

socially superior. This, at least, was the theory the police would begin to construct after the morning of Dec. 19, 1992, when one of those people, a 19-year-old man named David Rider, appeared in the alley and accepted Love's sexual invitation, even though by then Rider, whom police would characterize as "just a whore," had reached the conclusion, after a yearlong relationship, that Love was "a jerk."

33 Until then, however, there was very little reason to believe that the distinction Love made between his social ambitions and his sexual preferences — or, for that matter, between his past and his present — might turn out to be a fatal one. And though his friend Anthony Browne detected "a sadness in Kenneth" and knew about his "penchant for paying a hooker," neither the sadness nor the penchant seemed to deter Love from his course or from being a charming and thoughtful presence in his clients lives. If anything, the skillfulness with which he concealed the most elemental aspects of his life seemed to propel him faster and faster along.

34 With the success of his flower business, the Box Tree, Love was able to lease first a one-bedroom apartment in the Kennedy-Warren and then, in 1987, a larger one on the seventh floor with a view of Rock Creek Park. His friend Carl Draper helped him make the original move from Corcoran Street to Connecticut Avenue. "He had very little, maybe one room's worth of stuff," recalled Draper, now chief of food services for the Inter-American Development Bank. "So it was amazing to watch him begin to accumulate these incredible possessions. He had so many things sitting around, all sorts of heirloom silver and china that seemed to come from his grandmother and family."

35 By the beginning of the '90s, when he was inviting clients to tea and giving parties — which invariably included the sprinkling of red rose petals in the toilet — nobody would have thought Love was anything other than a happy, well-off man. He had applied all his energies to making the apartment feel intimate, much like the rooms of an Evelyn Waugh character, and although it was only a rental, he marbleized the

walls in the kitchen, hung wallpaper in the small library and chose a faded cabbage rose print by Geoffrey Bennison for the living room, which was more like a salon. On top of a large Empire table he placed ivy topiaries, silver candlesticks and stacks of books, upon which were framed pictures showing him with, among others, Queen Elizabeth when she was presented with a bouquet of his flowers at the Folger Library in 1991. In the bedroom, where the closet door had been faux-grained in salmon and green, there was a narrow bed — more like a day bed, really — and a high table set with picture frames and stacks of books, upon which rested a stone pineapple.

36 "He was haughty," said David Bell, who, as the owner of Mandrake in Georgetown, was probably Love's nearest rival in terms of floral style. Others saw Love as a social climber who would never reach the top rung. "Jennifer Phillips thought he was the best, but his clients would never invite him to table," said one interior designer, who did not want to be identified. "He was service."

37 Implicit in such comments, of course, is the double standard that makes it acceptable for one person to go up the ladder and not another, or, in this same insular frame of mind, for a white man, but not a black man, to live like "a well-bred gentleman." If Love sensed the exclusion, and Anthony Browne believed he did, then it might account for his ambivalent relations with whites as well as blacks. "He didn't socialize with black people at all," said Browne. "I think he felt that they didn't like him. On the other hand, if I gave a grand cocktail party, I'd suddenly be aware that Kenneth was in the back of the house. He was the florist." And it might explain his apparent need for embellishment — of his simple upbringing, his "heirloom" possessions and his relationship with David Rider, who quite possibly was the baby-faced "Davide" his friends recall meeting at a party at Love's within a year of his death. To Anthony Browne, the "only 'dark side' of Kenneth" was his preference for paying a hooker, which he attributed to Love's "great difficulty meeting people in a bar

or club." That he might have found a lover somewhere else was apparently not a possibility his friends considered.

38 None of this, however, was particularly interesting to the homicide detectives, who on the afternoon of Dec. 21, 1992, would begin to form a somewhat different impression of Love, one in which the physical evidence at the murder scene did not support a scenario of one-night stands. That the killer had been a friend was clear from his apparent knowledge of Love's apartment, although, in Rider's case, "friend" would turn out to be a fine distinction, for, as the detectives later discovered, he was supporting himself solely on the afterhours club scene. But it would also appear to the detectives that Love had led his friends to believe that his sexual encounters with hookers were strictly commerce, and therefore meaningless. "People form their opinions about you based on what you allow them to see," said Sergeant Walter Staples. "If his friends thought Kenneth was uncomfortable picking up men, I think that's what he wanted them to believe. I don't think this was a paying relationship. I think it was more of an established friendship."

39 After Love died, Oatsie Charles would try to fathom the difference between the man she thought she knew and the man he was. "This is what I can't get over," she said, her voice cracking. "How anyone as intelligent as Kenneth could allow this terrible degradation and humiliation and self destruction."

40 And so it was that on the afternoon of Dec. 21, the detectives began to construct a scenario of the events leading up to and including the murder of Kenneth P. Love, beginning with the morning of Dec. 18, when he rose early and went to the flower market. He put together 23 tulip arrangements for the Waltz Group's dinner dance at the Metropolitan Club that night, three more for a private party at Red Sage, and some sprays of holly and pine for a corporate dinner at the Phillips Collection. In the afternoon, he decorated a client's home for Christmas, picked up two cards from Oatsie Charles's maid to be delivered with flowers to Buffy Cafritz and Deeda Blair, and then returned to his studio at the flower mart, where he

loaded into his station wagon the arrangements he had made that morning. It was after 6 P.M. when he finished his deliveries.

41 Although he was expected at the Phillips dinner, he decided not to go, and went instead to a house-warming party for an employee of Anthony Browne. At 10:45 P.M., he left the party, saying he was going home, but went instead to Cafe Milano with a female friend. Shortly before midnight they went to Club Zei, where he remained until 2 the next morning, when he left and drove to the Fireplace on P Street. Around 3 A.M. he entered the alley outside the Fraternity House and saw David Rider standing there. According to the detectives, he asked Rider if he wanted to have sex with him. Rider declined. He asked Rider again a few minutes later and this time Rider said yes and got into the car. They drove to the Kennedy-Warren, entering through the garage, and went up to the seventh floor.

42 What happened after this point is a matter of speculation. There may have been a fight, as Rider's defense counsel, Stephen Russell, would contend at the preliminary hearing, and it may have been precipitated by Rider telling Love he was breaking off their relationship. Although the detectives saw no evidence of a struggle, Russell would contend that Love grabbed Rider by the wrists when he attempted to leave the apartment, and then kicked him in the groin. There is no dispute, however, about what happened next, because on Jan. 5, when Rider was charged with the murder of Love, he admitted, according to the detectives, that he had picked up the stone pineapple; struck Love in the face; cut his ankles and testicles; removed from the apartment five gold watches, several suits, ties, shoes, toiletries and a Polo bag; left through the garage in Love's car; and pawned three of the watches on Monday, Dec. 21, 1992, the day the body was discovered.

43 Rider is being held without bond in the District of Columbia Jail, awaiting trial.

44 There was no doubt in the minds of those who knew Kenneth Love that he had come exceedingly far for a man, any

man, who had recognized that his place in life could be neither of his parents' making nor limited by anything other than his imagination. But it would also become clear to them, once they had the facts, that they had not been wrong about Love — not about what they did know, the exquisite taste and impeccable manners, but about what they didn't know — and it raised a question as to whether they knew anything at all.

Annotations to *mr. love*

This narrative has 44 paragraphs, 197 sentences and 4,421 words. It has 4.5 sentences per paragraph and 22.4 words per sentence. On all of these parameters, it deviates from the standards I set in Chapter 1. It is longer than a typical magazine article, and it is extremely long for a newspaper story.

Even though I recommended in Chapter 1 that you strive for paragraph lengths of 1 to 1.5 sentences, here we see that ***Paragraph 2*** has 17 sentences — and it probably is the longest paragraph in this entire book. However, notice that it begins with a teaser that also functions as a topic sentence: *Something else surprised Detective Ray Crawford that afternoon.* This statement not only arouses suspense, but also sets the topic for the entire paragraph, which is devoted to explaining what surprised Detective Crawford.

Relative to the time identified in the lead, ***Paragraph 2*** shifts the reader backward in time, so it is an example of a *flashback*, and ***Paragraph 3*** brings us forward again. The specific dates and times allow us to reconstruct events in our minds.

Note the descriptive detail in many places, notably ***Paragraph 2*** — *an Empire table set with topiaries and silver-framed pictures, shades of beige with khaki swags over the windows*; ***Paragraph 15*** — *orchids and Rigaud candles and antique tables set with Limoges and silver flatware*; and ***Paragraph 35*** — *marbleized the walls, a faded cabbage rose print, faux grained in salmon and green.*

In view of the many shifts in time and location, transitions play a very important role in this story. Some of the transitions include *As it turned out* (***Paragraph 3***), *At Templeton* (***Paragraph 4***), *In Newport* (***Paragraph 5***), *On Dec. 26, at 2:30 P.M.* (***Paragraph 6***), *And as it turned out* (***Paragraph***

7), *In the spring of 1958* (***Paragraph 8***), and so on. Indeed, most of the paragraphs in this story open with transitional phrases.

In conclusion, what we see here is an entirely different kind of writing that opens up a new avenue of exploration for the daily journalist. If there are any cautionary remarks to be made here, one certainly stands out. The writer cannot successfully "mix and match" the various structures for news that have been presented so far. In other words, when approaching a news event, the writer should select the structure most suitable for relating the event to the reader and use it to the exclusion of others.

This leads us to another rule:

Rule No. 23:
Select a suitable structure and adhere to it.

The next structure, the Q-A story, is one of the most easily executed.

10

The Q-A Story

Q-A means *question-and-answer*. It refers to a common structure in journalism. There are two broad applications of the structure.

In the first application the Q-A structure is used to capture ***testimony in formal settings*** — courtrooms, councils, panels, legislatures and investigative bodies of all kinds. In this application, the Q-A matter is usually accompanied by an inverted pyramid.

In the second application, Q-A matter stands alone as a separate feature story. For this reason, I call it the ***Q-A feature***. The Q-A feature is a refreshing alternative to the inverted pyramid, which becomes stale with overuse.

Testimony in Formal Settings

In trials and hearings — and in interviews with powerful people on very sensitive topics — the precise phrasing of a person's remarks can be a matter of contention. Furthermore, in courtrooms and legislatures, the records of formal conversations are often preserved in public documents that are made available to the press.

For these reasons, reporting the exact words of the participants is at times the most simple and direct way to convey the facts.

There are two ways to do this: One is to write a ***Q-A sidebar*** to a regular inverted pyramid. The other is to open the story as usual — summary lead and supporting paragraph — and then provide a brief narrative explaining the circumstances leading to the Q-A sesssion. The writer can then proceed directly into a Q-A section without transition.

If you write a Q-A sidebar, then you should precede the Q-A matter with an ***editor's note***, like this:

Transcript of the Governor's Remarks

The interview with the Governor was conducted Monday afternoon in the west wing of Government House. Following is a full transcript of his remarks:

Question: How long can you postpone tabling of the democratic reform proposals without jeopardizing their implementation by the 1995 elections?

Answer: Obviously, for me to answer that question specifically would be to give a deadline for the proposals to be tabled, and I am loathe to do that as long as fruitful negotiations are being held with the opposition.

Q: There must be some point in time after which it will be too late, however. Why won't you discuss that time?

A: I won't discuss it for the reason that I just gave you. Meanwhile, you could probably estimate yourself when this time would be by studying the legislative and electoral process....

Notice that the words "question" and "answer" are followed by a colon, and they are abbreviated to "q" and "a" after their first use.

If you would like to build the Q-A session into the inverted pyramid itself instead of breaking it out as a sidebar, then you can do something along these lines:

Bosnia Leader Asks U.S. to Reject Plan

SARAJEVO, Bosnia-Herzegovina — President Alija Izetbegovic Monday asked the United States to reject the latest peace plan for Bosnia.

He said the accord endorses "ethnic cleansing" by the Serbian nationalists who have seized two-thirds of this former Yugoslav republic.

In a wide-ranging press conference with foreign journalists, Mr. Izetbegovic said the United States would be promoting a "huge tragedy" if it bowed to pressure from the United Nations and the European Community to endorse the accord.

> Mr. Izetbegovic, spontaneously switching back and forth from English to Serbo-Croatian, angrily attacked the authors of the peace plan, Cyrus R. Vance and Lord Owen, and Radovan Karadzic, leader of the Bosnian Serbs:
>
> *Question:* Will you be going to New York to lobby the United Nations on this issue?
>
> *Answer:* My place is here, not in New York, not in Washington.
>
> *Q:* Are you willing to meet again with Karadzic?
>
> *A:* Never again! They (Vance and Owen) forced me to sit at the same table with a man who inspired all these terrible crimes. Despicable is not too strong a word for a man like this....

As you can see from this example, an explicit transition is not needed between the inverted pyramid section and the Q-A section of the story.

In both examples above, notice that the words "question" and "answer" are set in a different typeface from the rest of the text. This makes it easier for the audience to read the story.

The Q-A Feature

With a small amount of enterprise and foresight, the journalist can execute a feature story in Q-A format. Here is a very clever example:

> **Cursors of Love Ne'er Did Run Smooth**[1]
>
> *By Jeff MacGregor*
>
> *New York Times Service*
>
> LOS ANGELES — Welcome to the Love-Maker! (v 3.1 Erosoft Industries, (C) 1993).
>
> At the prompt, please enter your response.
>
> I am the LOVEMAKER. A personalized interactive poetry assistance program. What is your name?
>
> JOHN
>
> What a nice name, JOHN. You must be a man.

[1] *International Herald Tribune*, Hong Kong, Tuesday, 16 February 1993, No. 34,203, p. 1.

YES

How nice for you. Who is your poem for, JOHN?

SHEILA

How nice for SHEILA. She must be a woman?

YES

SHEILA must be very special to you JOHN. Is she?

YES

What is the occasion, JOHN?

VALENTINE'S DAY

SHEILA is a very lucky woman. I will need information about SHEILA for a poem that best reflects your deep feelings for her, JOHN. What color are her eyes?

BLUE

Thank you, JOHN. But could you be more specific? Are they blue like the sky after a clearing storm? Are they the icy blue of the far-flung fjords, shrouded in mist and mystery? Are they the steely blue of Walter Gropius' later Bauhaus sketchbooks? Are they a cornflower blue that speaks of Sunday picnics in simpler times?

THEY LOOK KIND OF GRAY WHEN SHE'S ANGRY

Thank you, JOHN. What about SHEILA's hair?

BLOND

Thank you, JOHN. But could you be more specific? Is it ash blond with some auburn like the silky tresses of Rapunzel. When the sun hits it in a certain way in the late afternoon does it look like spun gold? Is it the hard, cheap blond of the street wise trollop or the dazzling, brilliant satin of Renaissance cherubim?

I THINK SHE DYES IT

Thank you, JOHN. Are there any other characteristics we should mention in our poem to SHEILA?

JOHN, are you still there?

SKIN?

Thank you, JOHN. But could you be more specific? Is it fine and alabaster and tightly grained like antique porcelain, slow-fired by master craftsmen? Or is it pink and lustrous like the Hand-burnished silver one's Grandmother might be found polishing with gentle, loving strokes on a rainy Sunday afternoon?

SHE TANS TWICE A WEEK

SHEILA must be very special to you, JOHN. You must have deep feelings for SHEILA to write her a special VALENTINE'S DAY poem.

YES

How nice for you, JOHN. What kind of poem to you think SHEILA would like?

?

My MENU (Alt+M) offers the following styles. At the prompt, please choose ONE:

couplet triplet quatrain eclogue pastoral sonnet elegy sextet epic ballad lyric ode idyll haiku blank verse

?

That's O.K., JOHN. How do you see yourself? Please choose ONE:

laureate bard lyricist sonneteer troubadour Meistersinger jongleur versifier minstrel rhapsodist Parnassian other (specify)

OTHER

Can you be more specific?

I GUESS....

Perhaps if you briefly shared your innermost dreams and desires, JOHN?

I'M THINKING

May I make a suggestion, JOHN?

SURE

Perhaps you imagine yourself a hopeless romantic, JOHN. A man who lives and loves with passion and desire and appetite. A man who grabs great platters from the groaning board of this world and eats his fill.

A man who takes what he wants the moment he sees it and makes it his own. A man who kneads fate in his strong hands, shapes it and commands it. A man with a reckless bent and the courage born of fire.

A man who sees beauty in a raindrop and all the truth of the universe in the eyes of a child. A man with needs and wants a flame within him. A man of power and means and influence, JOHN.

A man destined to be the envy of other men. A man that few can ever understand and fewer still will have the guts to love. A man of whom it might safely be said....

Would that Alexander in his age
had but half the measure of his strong
stout heart or
clear hawk's eye undimmed and true,
pooled with azure purpose. No earthbound mortal he,
but master o'er each and all....

Would that describe your self-image accurately, JOHN?

YES

I thought so. I'll use my random SEARCH MODE (Alt+S) to choose an appropriate style for you, JOHN. One that truly expresses your deep feelings for SHEILA on VALENTINE'S DAY. Please wait.

To print poem please enter command Alt+P at prompt.

Dear SHEILA,
Roses are red
Violets are blue
Your hair is blond
and your eyes are gray (when angry)
JOHN

Thank you for using LOVE-MAKER v 3.1 from EROSOFT.

Multiple Interviewees

All of the examples so far have been illustrations of Q-A stories with only a single interviewee, but this should not be considered a limitation. Q-A stories often include responses from several interviewees.

In the following example, you will see a single question posed to several interviewees. It also is an example of criticism, which will be discussed in more depth in Chapter 12.

Jackson fails to stay ahead of the trends[2]

The Guide received a copy of Michael Jackson's new album, Dangerous, *which will be in the shops on Tuesday. We asked MTV*

---

[2] *Sunday Morning Post*, 24 November 1991, p. 3, The Guide.

presenters, radio disc jockeys and record critics what they thought of Jackson's new look and sound:

Danny McGill, MTV presenter: The sound is harder than his previous recordings, and it is noticeable that Quincy Jones did not produce this album. The first half is hard dance music, with ballads following. Jackson has developed and changed his style with an album that is musically more daring, and, perhaps, more mature.

Rick O'Shea, Commercial Radio: I like the new single; it's fresh and immediate. We're giving it a lot of airplay, and we've had a lot of requests for it. I'm glad it's not mellow — it's still not a new sound, but he's not behind the trends, either. I was disappointed with his image — Madonna was right, he needs a new look. He's done the horror look, the street look, and he should have gone for a more classy approach.

Brent Anderson, music critic: *Dangerous* is infinitely better than 1987's *Bad*, but still not all that good. "Black or White" rocks playfully and the guitar shuffle of "Give in to Me" has a good kick, but bright spots like these are few. Most of the album bogs down in muddy, faceless dance raps.

Suzanne Miao, Post music critic: The single "Black or White" is brilliant and the video is superb, but the album is a disappointment overall. Many of the songs sound the same as each other and Michael doesn't seem to have progressed musically at all in the four years since *Bad* was released. *Off the Wall* and *Thriller* were totally different to the music that other people were producing at the time, but *Dangerous* sounds the same as everything people are doing now.

Although this example was based on a series of separate interviews, some Q-A stories with multiple interviewees will arrange for them all to come to a meeting. A journalist will moderate the meeting, asking the questions and thus controlling the direction of the discussion.

Using Tape Recorders

The Q-A interview is arguably the only circumstance that clearly calls for the use of a tape recorder. The reason for this is that quotations from the subject tend to be lengthy, direct quotes. They must be accurate.

Equipment failure cannot be tolerated. It happens that, after imposing on a community leader for an hour or two of his time, the journalist returns to the news organization and discovers that a tape recorder has malfunctioned. Few events are more mortifying that this. The journalist has two choices — reschedule the interview or cancel the story.

Rescheduling the interview would reveal the journalist's ineptitude, and the second time around the interview would be less spontaneous. Cancelling the story would seem odd to the subject.

To avoid these problems the journalist should test equipment thoroughly before leaving the office. Then, at the interview site, the journalist should test the equipment again under the conditions of the interview — record part of the conversation and then play it back. Finally, the journalist should take copious notes just in the event of equipment failure.

In short, the journalist should take every precaution. For more on the use of tape recorders, see Chapter 5.

Using the Telephone

Personal interviews are preferred for obvious reasons, but there is no reason why the Q-A story cannot be obtained by telephone.

In such case, the journalist may want to acquire telephone recording equipment and to acquaint himself with local laws on recording telephone conversations.

Some telephone recording equipment is very simple and inexpensive. A small suction cup microphone, available for sale at electronic equipment outlets, may be placed on the telephone receiver and plugged into a conventional audio cassette recorder. The journalist should experiment with this kind of equipment before relying on it, because the quality is highly variable, depending on the type of telephone and microphone used.

An alternative is automatic telephone answering machines. Many models have tapes that may record up to an hour of conversation, and the quality is consistently better than that obtained with a suction cup microphone.

With regard to local laws, it is generally allowable to record telephone conversations provided that both parties are aware that a recording is being made. Before the interview itself commences, a common practice is to inform the other party while the tape recorder is playing, like this:

> *This is Jeremy Leung on September 3, 1995, recording a telephone interview with Councillor Lee Yue Yan. Do you consent to this recorded interview, Mr. Lee?*

Once the subject's permission is obtained on tape, he cannot deny that the journalist informed him about the use of a recording device.

11

The Wall Street Journal Formula

This structure is named for one of the world's largest and most prestigious English language dailies, *The Wall Street Journal*. A regional edition, *The Asian Wall Street Journal*, is commonly available in Southeast Asia.

The reason the structure bears the name of the newspaper is that *The Wall Street Journal* perfected the formula, and there is a story written with this structure in almost every issue. In the newspaper's New York editorial offices, the structure is sometimes called the *evergreen formula*, because the stories written this way are "always green" — that is to say, fresh.

The formula itself has four parts, and they are easy to remember: (1) the story always opens with a focus on an individual; (2) then there is a transition to the main issue; (3) next there is the development of the main issue; and (4) finally there is a return to original focus.

Let's take them one at a time.

Focus on an Individual

This is the lead. It is usually an anecdotal lead about a person who represents the issue that the story is about. The lead may be up to four paragraphs long. The following lead is only one graf, however:

> SINGAPORE — When a 19-year-old Nanyang Technological University student posted an obscene email to a computer bulletin board at the University of Minnesota, he got a rude surprise: Nanyang administrators shut down his computer account and suspended him from the University for one academic term.

This story is about foul language and pornography on the Internet. It opens with a single case, focussing on an individual. The individual is invoked to illustrate the trend, as well as the potential consequences, of posting obscene email.

Once the example is established, the writer makes a transition to the main issue.

Transition to the Main Issue

This is a single paragraph. Aside from the lack of a date, and aside from the immediate identification, this transitional graf looks very similar to the summary lead on an inverted pyramid. It summarizes the problem and thereby identifies what the story is really about:

> Mr. Kot Tak Yin is one of some 50 million users of the Internet, most of whom have little understanding of the discretionary power of tens of thousands of system operators to monitor their communications. These system operators, or "sysops" in computer jargon, have the final say over who is censured, and why, in more than 100 countries.

At this point, the reader has a clear idea of where the story is going. The next step is development of the main issue.

Development of the Main Issue

The next stage, which is several paragraphs long, is the full treatment of the subject matter at hand.

This section of the story is written in inverted pyramid style, with material presented in descending order of importance.

> In fact, in most nations the technology of the Internet has leapfrogged ahead of the legislation governing it, so there are few laws regulating the posting of objectionable material.
>
> As a result, sysops everywhere are the final arbiters of what is acceptable — or unacceptable — on the nets....

Once the story has been fully written, the writer closes the story by returning to the original focus.

Return to Original Focus

This is usually a single paragraph, and it refers again to the person mentioned in the lead.

In the above example, the subject of the original focus was the 19-year-old Nanyang University student, so he is also the subject of the final graf:

> Said Nanyang University's Mr. Kot: "I am really sorry about all this. I had no idea the whole world was watching."

The strength of this kind of ending is that it provides clozure, a comfortable ending to the story — a resolution, if you will.

In the next section, a complete story is presented, with annotations.

condoms

The following piece, which was written by one of my students at The Chinese University of Hong Kong, is an illustration of a full story built according to the WSJ formula.

Condoms: The ultimate protection?[1]

By So Mei Chi

1 In a recent conversation about condoms, a 24-year-old salesgirl claimed that using condoms is simple.

2 "Everyone knows how to use them," she said, giggling. "It's not something that needs to be taught."

3 After several minutes of persuasion, she explained how a condom should be used. After opening the package, the user should unroll the condom before it is put on the penis, she said.

4 She was wrong, however. In fact, unrolling a condom before putting it on might rip or puncture the condom, according to the Family Planning Association. This can result not only in unwanted pregnancies, but also in the spread of sexually transmitted diseases.

---

[1] *Varsity* magazine, The Chinese University of Hong Kong, February 1994, p. 11.

5 Misinformation about the use of condoms is common. Although condoms are the most convenient way to have safe sex, not everyone knows how to use them. Besides, public information campaigns on the subject have drawn fire from critics.

6 Dr. Lee Shui Shan, a consulting physician in the AIDS prevention unit of the Health Department, put the situation like this:

7 "In theory, a physical barrier is 100 percent effective. However, the condom is not perfect, and this is due not only to the condom's design, but also the manner of usage," said Dr. Lee.

8 As if to underscore Dr. Lee's point, the data on pregnancy rates among condom users is high. The number of pregnancies "per 100 women years" among condom users is 10 to 20, compared to only 0.1 among women who use birth control pills or injections, according to the Family Planning Association. In other words, pregnancy rates for women who use condoms, as opposed to the pill, are at least 100 times higher.

9 Pregnancy rates for women who use other popular birth control methods are as follows:

10 • Intra-uterine devices, 1 to 3;

11 • Condoms with spermicide, 3 to 10;

12 • Diaphragms, 5 to 20;

13 • Spermicide, 20 to 25;

14 • Periodic abstinence, 25 to 30.

15 • The Health Department's Dr. Lee said ignorance by condom users is a problem that should be dealt with on a societal level.

16 "If sex is regarded as a 'dirty' thing in society which is indecent to be spoken out, how can our campaigns be legitimate?" he asked.

17 Some campaigns have run into trouble. A controversy has erupted over a 30-second television spot showing a scene of a man and a woman making love. The purpose of the spot was to promote the use of condoms.

18 "We planned the TV spot with the view that we should do more than just talking. The spot introduced clear concepts of safe sex and was in good taste," Dr. Lee said.

19 Though restricted to late night television, it has invited much criticism — even from the 24-year-old salesgirl.

20 "I think it is actually publicizing making sex instead of safer sex," said she.

Annotations to *condoms*

The individual that the lead focusses on in this story is the "24-year-old salesgirl", whose name was omitted deliberately in order to spare her any embarassment. The lead is four paragraphs — ***Paragraphs 1–4*** — which is a bit long, but is nevertheless effective.

Paragraph 5 is the transition to the main issue, which is misinformation in society about proper use of condoms. This paragraph looks very much like a *topic lead*, defined above, or a *summary lead* without a specific time or person to whom the information is attributed.

Paragraph 6 is the beginning of the development of the main issue, and to do this the writer quotes an authoritative source.

In ***Paragraph 8***, note the use of quotation marks in the expression "per 100 woman years". This is a way to signal the reader that you are quoting a technical expression, that it is not your own choice of words. Sometimes such a technique would be followed by a definition in plain English, but, in this case, the meaning should be evident to most readers.

Paragraphs 10–14 are a good example of how to provide a list for readers. The heavy black dots (•) are called ***bullets***. There is another example of the use of bullets in Chapter 4. Notice that each bullet precedes an ***elliptical phrase*** — that is, *a phrase with several words missing, but whose meaning is nevertheless clear.* Also, each phrase ends with a semicolon, except for the last, which ends with a full stop.

In ***Paragraph 15***, note the expression "the Health Department's Dr. Lee". This is a way to remind readers what agency Dr. Lee represents. This is a common technique if the last reference to a source is several paragraphs higher in the story. It is provided as a courtesy to readers so they will not have to go backwards in the story to refresh their memories.

Paragraph 16 provides an example of quotes within quotes, 'dirty'. The style is single quotes within double quotes. In this use, they indicate that the speaker himself does not believe sex is dirty.

The closing grafs, ***Paragraphs 19–20***, return to the original focus, the 24-year-old salesgirl.

This formula is remarkably similar to one used by *Time* magazine in reporting on social trends. I call the *Time* formula the *Time trend piece*, and it is discussed in Chapter 13, on Precision Journalism.

One of my acquaintances at *Newsweek* told me that his magazine uses a formula similar to the Time trend piece.

12

Criticism and Reviews

The critics at a newspaper — that is, the people who write reviews of cultural events — have coveted beats. These are the people who receive free tickets to orchestral performances, rock concerts, plays, and art shows. They are inundated with free books and compact discs from publishers hoping for favourable reviews. They get free meals when doing restaurant reviews.

Needless to say, they receive special treatment everywhere they go — the best seats, opening night parties, dress rehearsals and so on.

These perquisites raise a few ethical concerns, and they are discussed in Chapter 1 and in the Appendix; however, the point to be made here is that writing criticism and reviews is viewed by some as the ultimate journalistic assignment.

What is Reviewed?

Some of the obvious subjects for criticism and review are named above — theatre, concerts, art shows, books, compact discs and restaurants. Other topical areas include television and film. Nowadays it is fashionable as well to review videotapes, even though they usually are released several months after the original films open in the moviehouses — and several months after the films have been critiqued in the newspapers.

And now that computer hardware and software is converging with conventional entertainment media, we are beginning to see reviews of computer software in the newspaper.

The creative reviewer will not stop with this list, however. Museums, wines, fashions.... Almost any "cultural" product or event, loosely defined, may be subject to a critique. Here is part of a review of an amusement park:

American Family at Euro Disney[1]

By William E. Schmidt
New York Times Service

1 PARIS — Somewhere deep inside the pirate's cave, beneath a jagged ceiling of simulated stalactites, we were marooned. After plunging down pitch-black flumes and dodging grapeshot and curses from angry French sea rovers, the little parade of mechanical boats curling through Euro Disney's Pirates of the Caribbean had thumped, quite suddenly, to a stop.

2 On one side of us, a pirate's skull, covered in cobwebs, grinned wickedly. On the other, a ghostly harpsichord played over and over and over again the opening bars of the same agonizingly familiar Disney chantey.

3 "Yo ho, yo ho, it's a pirate's life for me," we hummed along helplessly, as the seconds stretched into minutes and Euro Disneyland's French technicians plotted our rescue from a mechanical failure.

4 My wife, Margo, our three children and I had arrived at the park, near Marne-la-Vallée, about 30 kilometers east of Paris, only a half hour earlier, having set out from our small hotel near the Eiffel Tower at an ambitious 7:30 A.M. At the turnstiles, the cheerful young attendants had wished us all "a Disney Day." Now, in the five minutes our boat bobbed aimlessly inside the cave, I turned to Lindsay, my 12-year-old daughter, and remarked, with fatherly irony, "This is just great, isn't it?" She looked past me, at the dripping stone walls and pirate's skeleton spookily straddling a mound of golden coins and plundered booty.

5 "Un-unh," she corrected me. "This place is awesome."

6 For 13 hours that first day, and five hours the next, we encountered a lot of other bumps and bugs at Disney's new European resort: ice cream bars that cost nearly $3 apiece,

---

[1] *International Herald Tribune*, Hong Kong, Friday, 29 May 1992, No. 33,980, p. 10.

unruly lines, moving sidewalks that did not move and attractions and rides plagued by what attendants always politely described as "technical difficulties."

7 Twice, we were turned out of line at the Pinocchio ride in Fantasyland because it was not working. Later, we arrived at Star Tours, the spectacular George Lucas attraction imported from Disney-MGM Studios in Florida, to find staff members waving people away. Over their shoulders we could see water streaming from a concrete planter and forming a growing pool across the entrance.

8 It was barely a month after Euro Disney's opening in mid-April, and the park had the feel of a work in progress: Its stringy trees and fresh landscaping gave it the look of a new subdivision, and its young staff was still trying to master the demands of its multilingual audience. (The young French woman on duty at the Frontierland petting zoo only shrugged when we asked her about the hog-calling contest, advertised on the park sign next to her. Clearly, this was one arcane bit of English she had not yet mastered.)

9 But for all that, our children — Lindsay, her 15-year-old sister, Jordan, and their 7-year-old brother, Peter — were untroubled.... "This was the best day of my whole life," Peter later pronounced to no one in particular, shortly before he dropped off to sleep.

Annotations to *euro disney*

The original review was quite long, more than 2,000 words, but it would have answered an important question for most families planning to tour Paris: Should we, or should we not, include a visit to Euro Disney as part of the itinerary?

Note that ***Paragraph 1*** is an anecdotal lead in the first person. Using the first person is appropriate here because the writer is engaging in ***participant observation*** — a journalistic term meaning that he is participating in events in order better to report about them. Participant observation is discussed more fully in the next chapter.

Notice the explicit detail in ***Paragraphs 1*** and ***2***. ***Paragaraph 4*** opens with a transition explaining how the family had come to be at Euro Disney in the first place.

Paragraph 5 contains the expression *un-unh*, an interjection denoting disagreement.

The author uses wry humour in ***Paragraph 8*** when he refers to the "hog-calling contest", an event popular at fairs in rural America.

In the opening paragaraphs, the author has made it obvious that the review will be unfavourable, and he supports this view with specific observations — rides do not function, attractions are closed to the public. However, he provides balance in ***Paragraphs 5*** and ***9***, where we see his children disagreeing with his assessment.

In short, when you are doing a review, you should establish a clear position and support it with specific information.

How to Plan a Film Review

The way a review is done will depend largely on the subject. Reviewing a film is quite unlike reviewing a restaurant, for example. For this reason, the best way to plan a review is to create a checklist of items that should come under scrutiny.

For a film review, here are some suggestions:

- ***Technical aspects***: These include photography, editing, set design, lighting, and sound. Is the film in black and white? If so, is it effective? Do scenes follow one another in a logical order? Are there flashbacks? Are there lots of "location" shots?
- ***Artistic aspects***: These include screenplay, acting, musical score, directing, and costumes. Is the dialogue natural? Do the actors look like they are acting, or is the acting transparent? If the film is a period film, are the costumes authentic?
- ***Business aspects***: These include distribution, market response, production costs and backers. How much did the film cost to make? How much money is being spent on distribution? Are the theatres sold out?
- ***Historical aspects***: These include the genre, the successes and failures of the director and leading actors, and sequels. Is it a western, a

psychological thriller or science fiction? Does the director have a proven record of success in this genre?

Television Criticism

If television shows are shallower than films, then a corollary might be that television criticism is shallower than film criticism. Of course, this is an overgeneralization that is becoming less true as television matures as a medium.

In any case, it is fair to say that television criticism tends to focus on the here-and-now of day-to-day TV programming, and it is directed at the television audience — that is, an audience that is largely uncritical of the medium itself.

For this reason, television criticism tends to be informational and entertaining, requiring little or no specialized knowledge of the reader. Typically, it consists largely of gossip about TV personalities and industry leaders, the strengths and weaknesses of the daily program lineup, and topical matters such as implications in the shifts in TV station ownership and management.

Occasionally, there are more serious reviews of specific shows as well. A *review* should not be confused with a *preview*, however. A ***preview*** is an announcement of an upcoming show or series, usually including enough detail about the plot to arouse interest without destroying the suspense. A ***review***, on the other hand, is a look back at previously aired shows, essentially containing a series of evaluative statements supported mainly by details drawn from the shows themselves.

The review is meaningful principally because it is published before the series ends. Thus, viewers who have not seen early episodes may become interested enough to tune in to later ones.

Perhaps the most sophisticated reviews are done on so-called ***mini-series***, a 2-, 3-, or 4-episode show that runs on consecutive nights or on the same night in consecutive weeks. Mini-series are high-budget projects with a lot of ***talent*** — that is, experienced writers, directors and actors.

Mini-series are distinguished from ***episodic series***, which are the most common kind of series on television. Episodic series, such as *Star Trek*, are made in half-hour or one-hour ***segments*** that may be run in any sequence because each show may stand alone as a separate story. Being able to air the segments in any order is one of the strengths of the episodic series — and it is one of the chief characteristics distinguishing them from mini-series. In a mini-series, the segments must be run in a specific sequence in order for the plot to unfold naturally.

Once an episodic series is shown, it is not shelved indefinitely. If there is any likelihood of selling it to other broadcasters, then it will be ***syndicated***. Syndicated shows are very common in Southeast Asia, most of them coming from the United States and Great Britain. They are easy for reviewers to write about, because they have a history. Many episodes will have been reviewed previously, so the writer has a precedent to draw on.

Book Reviews

Major news organizations receive a flood of books from publishers seeking reviews in the media. Few newspapers have full-time staff who write nothing but book reviews, however.

Nevertheless, many newspapers have writers who volunteer to write reviews on an irregular basis. If a local writer produces an interesting work that is unlikely to be reviewed by a major syndicate, then it probably should be featured some way in the local newspaper.

In my experience, there was always someone on the staff who wanted to review a book from time to time, and the editors permitted this, especially if a local writer was involved. Normally, such reviews were printed on Sundays, sometimes in the newspaper's Sunday magazine.

In any case, it was not a full time responsibility.

true life

Most book reviewers review the text itself without venturing beyond it. However, they might provide context by identifying the genre and the book's place in the author's overall body of work. Such reviews are a bit wooden, and so are boring to read. But they need not be this way. The following review, for example, required the reviewer to visit the author in his home and conduct an interview with him. The details from the interview are interwoven with the context of the author's life:

True Life: The Best-Seller From Nowhere[2]

By William Souder

Washington Post Service

1 CEDAR FALLS, Iowa — In the summer of 1990, Robert James Waller — then a 50-year-old economics professor and sometime folk musician — was on his way home to Cedar Falls after a day of photographing the old covered bridges of Madison County, southwest of Des Moines.

2 Driving through the heat, Waller says he began to hear a line from a song he'd been working on recently, "an old bossa nova tune", about a woman named Francesca. He got to wondering about her. What if Francesca lived in Iowa? And what if she met a man, a man named — Robert? Robert Kincaid. Back home, Waller began to write his first novel, which would become, by early this year, the best-selling work of fiction in the United States. He says he didn't stop writing, except to eat and sleep, for 14 days. "I never wanted it to end."

3 The book is a spare but emotional short novel, "The Bridges of Madison County," about a 45-year-old Iowa farm wife and her four-day affair with a 52-year-old photographer from National Geographic. Despite their brief time together, Francesca and Robert fall into a transcendent, slow-moving spiral of courtship, love and mutual seduction. Then they part, never to see each other again.

4 With help from friends, Waller secured an agent in New York. "The Bridges of Madison County" was sold to Warner Books, and the film rights were optioned to Steven Spielberg. An initial printing of 20,000 copies arrived in bookstores last April.

5 At first the book sold slowly. But then smaller, independent booksellers across the country fell in love with it and

---

[2] *International Herald Tribune*, Hong Kong, Thursday, 11 February 1993, No. 34,199, p. 18.

began urging their customers to buy it. As spring gave way to summer, "The Bridges of Madison County" was turning into one of the most successful word-of-mouth books ever published. The Washington Post lamented the book's "triteness," the Los Angeles Times likened Waller's story to a "Coke that's been opened a while ago: sweet but flat." A more typical reaction was that of the Orlando Sentinel, who called the book "as perfect as a tear."

6 In August, "The Bridges of Madison County" made The New York Times best seller list, where it has since remained. For the past two Sundays it's been No. 1, having sold some 420,000 copies after 19 printings.

7 If Spielberg were casting the movie today, he'd find the prototype for Robert Kincaid in the soft-spoken man who answers the door at a modest A-frame in a secluded neighborhood. Robert James Waller is 53. He stands 6 feet 1 and is arrestingly thin but fit-looking. He is a vegetarian who smokes cigarettes and also jogs. He is partial to jeans and cowboy boots. "I come back into fashion about every five years," he says.

8 Waller has a sturdy ego. He says he based Robert Kincaid on himself, and Francesca, to a lesser extent, on his wife, Georgia Ann, a striking, dark-haired woman to whom he has been married for 31 years.

9 The story is told mainly from Francesca's point of view. In various places in the story Robert is called a gazelle, a leopard and "a star creature who had drifted in on the tail of a comet." He makes love like a wild animal, except he takes his time. Robert believes he's the end of an evolutionary chain that began in the Stone Age and is now winding down in Francesca's upstairs bedroom. As they make love, Robert says to Francesca, "I am the highway and a peregrine and all the snails that ever went to sea." But for all its gibberish about ancient evenings and faraway places, the book is vividly romantic. It's racy in a deft manner — explicit without being specific. If he's not the best of writers, Waller is nonetheless an amazing storyteller, skillful in the ways that tend to matter

most to readers. The book moves ahead relentlessly, but the speed is deliberate and the movements are gradual.

10 It all started, in a way, back in 1985, when Waller was dean of the business school at the University of Northern Iowa. He felt overworked and worried about some investments in which he was sure he was being swindled, and he suffered a "fatigue-stress" attack. He had to quit his job. "It gives you all the symptoms of a heart attack except without the pain," he says. For the next six years or so, he says he just drifted, writing essays for the Des Moines Register, playing music, taking photographs and teaching a few courses.

11 Waller is a publisher's dream. With one book at the top of the best-seller list, he has two more completed. "Slow Waltz in Cedar Bend," another romance, will be published in the fall. "I think Warner wanted 'Robert and Francesca II,'" he says. After that Waller hopes to bring out "Puerto Vallarta Squeeze," a thriller that's not only different in content but very different stylistically — filled with stream-of-consciousness narration and hard-boiled dialogue. Waller says he rarely bogs down when writing.

12 The success of "The Bridges of Madison County" has given the Wallers a financial freedom they scarcely envisioned just a year ago, when they tapped their retirement account for $100,000 so Robert could continue writing. "I suppose we could travel," says Waller, considering some of their favorite places. "We could go to Paris. Or somewhere warm — Georgia hates winter. We could go to India for six months."

13 Waller bristles at the charge of excessive sentimentality that has been the principal criticism of the book. "Sure there's a line you can cross," he says. "I plead guilty to falling on the wrong side of it at times. There are some things in the book that make me cringe a bit. I mean, some of it is way out there. I do get sentimental. But why is that an indictment? I am a sentimentalist, and I take a beating for it, especially from academics. Of course, I have no faith in academics, having been one myself for 25 years."

14 Maybe when the fuss dies down, Waller will find himself alone again and back in the place he started, no matter where he happens to be. He conveys a sense of being a man still on intimate terms with the boy he was. It's cold and empty out here right now, and Waller is working on the next installment of his own romantic education, one arriving in bookstores everywhere soon.

Annotations to *true life*

Note that ***Paragraph 5*** cites other reviewers. Obviously the reviewer has researched his subject. And because the novelist himself lives far from a major news organization, the reviewer must have travelled a great distance to get a personal interview at his residence, alluded to in ***Paragraph 7***. During the interview, the reviewer confronts the novelist about some of the criticism he has received and elicits his response, provided in ***Paragraph 13***.

If there is a lesson to be learned from this book review, it's that the reviewer need not feel constrained to sit in his office and write a review based strictly on the text. A chat with the author may enliven and enrich the review, perhaps even bring it to life.

13

Precision Journalism

In Chapter 1 I mentioned that *objectivity* is a central concept in modern journalism. I also drew a parallel between science and journalism, claiming that the two fields have much in common. For example, both observe and report empirical events to a wide audience.

Recent decades have witnessed an emergence of increased scientific rigour in journalism. This is due in part to empirical research programmes in the journalism schools at some major American universities — notably the University of Wisconsin, the University of Minnesota, the University of Indiana and Stanford University.

The result has been the development of a new concept in newsgathering, precision journalism. ***Precision journalism*** is *the use of scientific research methods to collect and report news*. The methods come from the social sciences — sociology, anthropology, psychology, economics, geography. Indeed, it was the introduction of this "social scientific" component to journalism education that caused journalism departments to be located within social science faculties at major universities around the world, including some in Southeast Asia.

The most common kind of story that uses social science research methods is the public opinion poll. Such polls are commonly commissioned by news organizations. Governments, universities, political groups and private agencies also conduct polls and report their findings to the news media in press releases and press conferences.

As a result, in modern urban societies today news organizations frequently report the results of such polls. So it is incumbent on them to understand how such polls are conducted and to report the results fairly.

In order to put the discussion in perspective, however, it is important to make a distinction between qualitative and quantitative research methods.

Quantitative versus Qualitative Techniques

Quantitative techniques are numeric and they require statistics; ***qualitative techniques*** are nonnumeric and they do not require statistics.

The professional journalist is ably equipped to conduct qualitative research, which relies heavily on interviewing and personal observation. Psychoanalyst Sigmund Freud and anthropologist Margaret Mead were adept practitioners of qualitative methods. Mead's relatively small number of in-depth interviews with young Samoans revealed that sexual customs were culture-bound, a conclusion believed to set in motion a sexual revolution in the United States. Ironically, however, her 50-year-old findings were challenged recently by an Australian anthropologist who attempted a replication of her work using quantitative methods. His data did not support Mead's principal findings, but her stature in anthropology is not disputed.

Qualitative methods also have applications in the natural sciences — zoology and botany, for example. Practitioners include Charles Darwin, Konrad Lorenz, Diane Fossey, and Jane Goodall. Most of Darwin's research on evolution was qualitative, as were Lorenz's and Fossey's research on animal behaviour. Primatologist Goodall, in her continuing studies of chimpanzee society in the mountains of Gambia, relied heavily on detailed observation rather than numerical analysis.

Quantitative methods rely less on personal observation. Instead, all observations are collapsed into numerical categories, and these are then subject to statistical analysis. Many people are intimidated by the prospect of collecting and analyzing numerical information, but there is no need to be: The common methods of data analysis are few in number, easily executed, and thoroughly described in dozens of common reference books. These numerical calculations may be done on computers or on hand-held calculators.

Research combining both qualitative and quantitative methods is called ***thick data collection***, and many scientists assert that this is the ultimate in observation techniques.

Qualitative Techniques

Three common qualitative techniques will be introduced here — the oral history, the case study, and participant observation.

Oral history is the tape recording of reminiscences of recent historic events by participants and witnesses. This was done recently in Europe when, on the 50th anniversary of V-E Day, which is the day Germany surrendered to the Allies near the end of World War II, journalists interviewed people who witnessed the events of that time.

With this practice, journalists transform their craft into that of historiographers, or writers of history. As a research method, it is only about 30 years old, its birth coinciding with the wide diffusion of portable tape recorders. It probably is most effective when used to recount the activities of individuals involved in an event whose historical significance was not evident at the time. For example, the crews who flew with General Doolittle in the bombing raids on Japan, or Chinese Communist Party cadre who participated in the Long March, would be likely candidates for oral histories.

The formal steps in a complete oral history are the following: preinterview preparation, the interviews themselves, between-interview research, and transcription.

As part of preinterview preparation, the journalist should familiarize himself or herself as much as possible with the subject and create a list of potential topics for discussion. The journalist also should arrange a preinterview meeting. Here the journalist should establish rapport with the subject and set the parameters for the interviews themselves. If feasible, the journalist may request borrowing personal effects — copies of speeches or newspaper clippings, for example — that would aid in the background research. Other points that should be covered in the preinterview meeting are basic biographical information and the legalities of the interview. For book-length projects, the use of transcribed conversations may require a signed legal release that assigns literary and property rights to the tapes and transcripts. The journalist should seek an unconditional release, but the subject may seek to impose certain restrictions.

In order to minimize the imposition on the subject, the interviews should be few in number — no more than half a dozen — and to avoid fatigue, they should not last longer than 90 minutes each. Also, they should take place in the subject's home, if possible. This will make the subject feel comfortable and permit access to historic materials.

During the interviews, the journalist should follow tips given in Chapter 6 on interviewing techniques: Encourage the subject by maintaining eye contact, nodding, and giving other affirmative responses. During long pauses after questions, the journalist should resist the temptation to speak and allow the subject time to reflect on the response.

The interviews themselves should be guided by a list of questions or topics based on the preinterview preparation, and these should be organized in outline form. The journalist should not attempt to correct, debate, or educate the subject; discrepancies and apparent errors of fact should be the subject of between-interview research, and unresolved issues should be dealt with as follow-up questions in subsequent interviews.

For equipment, all that is needed is a good tape recorder, an extension cord, plug adaptors, several tapes, pens, and notepads. The notepad should be used for recording the position of the tape for reviewing responses to important questions between interviews. The notepad also is useful for recording nonverbal responses. During the transcription, notations for long pauses, smiles, and other nonverbal responses may be inserted in the text.

Following the transcription, the journalist should audit the transcribed material by reading over the transcribed text while replaying the tapes.

Interviews of this depth are rarely if ever done for daily print media; however, a scaled-down version may provide interesting opportunities for the creative journalist.

The ***case study*** technique was used successfully by Karl Marx and Sigmund Freud, and it still is utilized by scholars on the European Continent. It fell out of favour in the United States with the growth of positivistic methods, inherited from Great Britain, but it nonetheless has applications in journalism.

In the case study, the social scientist attempts to study a social phenomenon by examining people or organizations that represent it. Examples in news media have been feature stories about individuals with AIDS. Serialized versions of these in newspapers have in some cases followed the patients to their deathbeds — and been especially poignant as a result.

The case study is similar to the oral history in requiring elaborate preparation for in-depth interviews. The principal difference is in its objective: The oral history is a technique to write history, while the case study is a technique to demonstrate a social phenomenon by means of illustration with one or more cases.

In the best kind of case study, there is more than one subject. Individuals selected for study are picked to represent variations of the phenomenon, and the selection is designed to maximize the comparisons among one another. If groups most affected by AIDS are male homosexuals, intravenous drug users, offspring of intravenous drug users, and hemophiliacs, then a newspaper series on the social effects of AIDS might include a representative of each group.

In ***participant observation*** the social scientist pretends to be a participant in events while taking notes and keeping a sense of objectivity. It is not rare for journalists to use this method for spying on clandestine organizations; however, in going undercover they clearly misrepresent themselves and engage in deceptive practices.

This raises ethical issues in the minds of some journalists. Indeed, the Hong Kong Journalists Association prohibits this practice unless it is necessary to get the story — that is, if there is no other way to tell the story than by subterfuge.

Quantitative Techniques

Quantitative techniques may be broken down into experiments and field surveys, also known as polls. Experiments are too technical for the journalist without special training.

Field surveys usually are *a sampling of public opinion*, such as how people intend to vote. Several kinds of these figure prominently in contemporary journalism — call-in polls, mail-in questionnaires, man-in-the-street interviews, straw polls, and randomly conducted interviews.

Most of these are methodologically unsound. A ***call-in poll***, for example, *asks respondents to telephone a number at a news organization* and *to vote one way or another on an issue*. Some newspapers ask respondents to dial one number if they approve of a proposition, or another number if they disapprove. Naturally, there is no way to control the voting process, so one individual can vote as many times as he or she desires.

In spite of the obvious ways in which such a poll can be abused, call-in polls are enormously popular in some urban areas, where they generate tens of thousands of calls from readers and viewers.

Mail-in questionnaires usually *request that readers clip a questionnaire printed in a newspaper or magazine, fill in answers, and mail it back to the publication.* This process faces some of the same methodological problems of the call-in poll: One person or a group of people can send in several questionnaires, biasing the results. Of greater concern is the fact that people who take the time to clip the questionnaire from the paper, fill it out, address an envelope, and mail it are not representative of the general population. Typically the respondents are retired or unemployed individuals who have extra time on their hands.

Man-in-the-street interviews usually are conducted to *get quotes that characterize public reactions to some event*, and half a dozen interviews are usually sufficient for this purpose. Naturally, such a small sample of opinion cannot be representative of the population as a whole.

Straw polls are *unofficial canvasses of the electorate to determine the popular sentiment on public issues* or candidates for office. One of the most famous of these was the National Popcorn Poll in the United States, which was conducted every four years by popcorn magnate Jim Blevins of Nashville, Tennessee. During American presidential election years, Blevins Popcorn Company, a major supplier of popcorn to movie theatres and stadiums, offered patrons a choice between a "Democratic box" and a "Republican box". In tabulating the returns, Blevins accurately predicted the outcomes of every presidential election from 1944 to 1980, when the inn was sold and the poll discontinued.

This is the origin of the term ***popcorn poll***, which means *an informal canvass of public opinion.*

These examples of inferior polls are presented in order to alert you to their existence — and to their shortcomings. When conducted in a rigorous scientific fashion, polls can be truly representative of public opinion.

Scientific Polling Techniques

It is highly unlikely that you will actually design a public opinion poll. But if you become an editor someday, it is possible there will be a time when you will have to work with a pollster in contracting for a poll or in reporting poll results. For this reason, some understanding of polling techniques is extremely valuable.

In order for a poll to be representative, the respondents must be selected at ***random***. This means that there must be equal likelihood that any person would be picked over any other person in the population. For example, if the population is 10,000, then there is equal likelihood of selecting John Doe or John Q. Public, and that likelihood is 1 in 10,000. A sample such as this based on probabilities is sometimes called a ***probability sample***.

Occasionally it is appropriate to oversample the number of people in a particular group in order to get a larger number of them for the analysis. In a metropolitan area with a population that is 20 percent foreign workers, a random sample of 1,000 people would include only about 200 foreign respondents. If the journalist wanted to estimate the attitudes of foreign workers in particular, then that part of the sample should be increased to at least 400. This is known as ***purposive sampling***.

The ***population*** is the group under study. For forecasts of election results, the population is ordinarily defined as people who satisfy the criteria to be registered to vote and who intend to vote in the election. If the date of the election is so close that it is too late to register to vote, then the population should be defined as people who are in fact registered to vote and who intend to vote in the election.

*The **sampling frame*** is the set of records used to pick people randomly for the poll. Census tracts and telephone books are common sampling frames.

The ***unit of analysis*** is the thing that the pollster is measuring. The voter is the unit of analysis in an election poll; the household is the unit of analysis in a general social survey.

Sample size is the number of respondents. For public opinion polls, sample sizes tend to range from 400 to 2,500. The latter figure is more than adequate for most purposes, regardless of the size of the population.

For practical purposes, the representativeness of the sample is not greatly increased by increasing its size. This is true regardless of the size of the population — and it's a concept that seems to contradict common sense.

For example, a random sample of 1,000 respondents in a city of 500,000 is as accurate as a random sample of 1,000 respondents in a country of 250 million. Although this can be proven mathematically, to do so is beyond the scope of this book.

This statement does not hold true for small populations.

Reporting Poll Results

Everyone can think of instances when polls were incorrect, and for this reason the public mistrusts news stories based on polls. The problem is exacerbated by politicians who, unhappy with the poll findings, publicly express contempt for poll results.

Because some of the inaccuracies are due to incorrect reporting of the findings, journalists have some control over the public's attitude toward polling. Correct interpretation of the findings will result in fewer complaints and less mistrust.

Guidelines for reporting poll results are published by the American Association for Public Opinion Research and the National Council on Public Polls. In general, these organizations recommend that news stories based on opinion polls include the following information:

- The name of the sponsoring organization;
- The date or dates of the poll;
- The manner in which interviewing was done, usually either by telephone or face-to-face;
- The manner in which respondents were chosen;
- The exact wording of key questions;
- The total number of respondents;
- The number of people in any subsample on which a result is based.

The importance of this last item is easily illustrated. If a random sample of 1,250 people reveals that 83 percent of all females favour abortion rights, then it is likely that this finding is really based on a sample of only about 625 people, which is the proportion of females that one would expect to find in a random sample of the population.

The reporter also should tell the reader what the *margin of error* was. The preceding example will serve as an example of how to report the margin of error. If the study actually polled 625 women, the margin of error would be almost 4 percent. And if 83 percent favoured abortion rights, then the actual figure would most likely lie in the range from 79 to 87 percent, which is 83 plus and minus 4 percent.

"Most likely" in the last sentence is a necessary qualification because of something called the confidence level. The concept comes from probability theory and its origins are somewhat esoteric for this book. Suffice it to say that statisticians usually work with 95 or 99 percent confidence levels.

Statisticians never expect things to come out perfectly. In 384 flips of a coin, for example, it is highly unlikely that there would be 192 heads, or exactly half. The figure very likely would be near 192, however, and the degree to which statisticians are confident of this is called the ***confidence level*** or ***confidence interval***. When it comes to actual figures for coin-tossing, in fact, a statistician would predict the following: 95 times out of 100, when flipping a coin 384 times, the number of heads will range from 173 to 211. Note that the figures 173 and 211 are derived from the margin of error for a sample of 384 — 5 percent of 384 is 19, and this was added and subtracted to 192.

In order to increase the confidence level to 99 percent, the statistician would have to increase either the error or the sample size. In reporting a poll result, therefore, some journalists include a reference to the confidence level. The language used to report the confidence level usually looks like this: "If the election were held today, chances are 95 out of 100 that the results would fall within the margin of error."

Increasing the sample size is costly, however. As the sample size increases from 100 to 500, the error is cut by 5.5 percent, more than half; however, as the sample size increases from 2,000 to 5,000, the error is cut by less than 1 percent. In other words, there are diminishing returns as the sample size increases, making very large samples impractical from a financial and logistical standpoint.

Social Indicators

The most common kind of survey reported by news media is the public opinion poll. But this is certainly not the only kind available to the journalist. Most developed countries conscientiously compile ***social indicators***, which are *statistics that enable policymakers to measure a society's progress in relation to its goals and objectives.*

These excellent sources of news are probably among the least utilized of all major sources, and they are among the easiest to obtain and write about.

Some common examples of social indicators are the infant mortality rate, the literacy rate, the average life expectancy, the amount of disposable personal income, the number of doctors per 1,000 population, the number of telephones per 1,000 population, and so on. These figures are available in public libraries and many government agencies.

In fact, there are hundreds, if not thousands, of such measures, and they often are grouped into broad categories. *System performance indicators* are measures of expenditures on major programmes and the results of the expenditures. For example, the amount of money spent on higher education, as opposed to the number of degrees awarded, is a measure of the performance of the educational sector. *Indicators of personal well-being* include crime rates, inflation, unemployment, and infant mortality. *Indicators of public perceptions* include measures on people's attitudes toward their own quality of life, their personal satisfaction with their own employment and educational level, and their trust of government and sense of political efficacy.

As mentioned above, these kinds of data are among the easiest to obtain and to write about. One of the best structures for reporting these data is the *Time trend piece*, perfected by *Time* magazine.

cohabitate: An Example of the *Time* Trend Piece

This structure is very similar to The Wall Street Journal formula, presented in Chapter 11. Like the WSJ formula, it has four parts: (1) the story opens with an anecdote that illustrates a trend; (2) then statistics such as social indicators are presented that establish the trend; (3) then there is speculation by experts who attempt to explain the trend; and (4) finally there is a kicker that, preferably, alludes to the original anecdote.

Here is a short, but complete, example of how the structure looks as a full news story:

Sexual Attitudes Changing:
Young Couples Have More Liberal Attitudes

By Wong King Wai

1 Mr. and Mrs. Lam Kwok Lee "didn't think it would happen." They knew that young people's sexual attitudes were undergoing some changes, but they did not know that the

change would affect the dynamics of their own family. Over breakfast last Sunday, however, their eldest daughter, Lam Mei Yan, announced that she was moving out of their flat and moving in with her boyfriend. Forthwith.

2 Their 19-year-old daughter's decision has caused acute embarrassment for the Lams. Being from another generation, they do not know how to explain the situation to friends and relatives. They resent their daughter's abrupt decision on the matter, which they believe has brought shame on the entire family.

3 In fact, 26 percent of Hong Kong residents now approve of cohabitation before marriage, according to a recent social survey conducted by the Hong Kong Institute for Asia-Pacific Studies. And another 17 percent said they would accept cohabitation "under some circumstances". The figures represent a marked increase over the figures only four years ago, and experts predict that it will continue to increase.

4 "Hong Kong is becoming increasingly urban and modern," said Prof. Lau Tak Yin of The Chinese University of Hong Kong. "One of the results of the increase in modernity is postponement of marriage, for a number of reasons.

5 "Some people postpone marriage to further their education. Others, especially women, see increased professional opportunities, so they postpone marriage in order to explore career possibilities."

6 Other factors include influences from the West, the availability of birth control pills, and smaller, less cohesive families, said Dr. Lau, a sociologist.

7 Whether the trend is favorable or not is a matter of debate. While some experts see it as an inevitable byproduct of modernity, others perceive a decay in the moral fiber of Hong Kong youth.

8 Among them is Legislative Councillor Wong Wai King, who has proposed tightening the laws on cohabitation.

9 "We must remember that what distinguishes Chinese people from Westerners is that sense of sexual propriety in marriage and family. We cannot forfeit this trait without

losing our Chinese-ness, so to speak. If we want to preserve our culture, we must address these lapses in morality."

10 Miss Wong has introduced a private member's bill into the Legislative Council that would require a couple that has cohabited for more than five days to be automatically declared "common-law husband and wife". Under her proposal, they would be declared married, whether they liked it or not, and they could not marry again without going through a formal divorce.

11 Meanwhile, they would be subject to all government regulations of ordinary married couples.

12 To Mr. and Mrs. Lam, all of this talk about new laws is far removed from their most immediate concerns — their daughter's intransigence.

13 "We just wish she would forget about this foolishness and come home," lamented Mrs. Lam.

Annotations to *cohabitate*

The anecdote that illustrates the trend is presented in ***Paragraphs 1–2***. The poignancy of the story immediately grips the reader. ***Paragraph 3*** identifies the trend by citing social indicators data. Note that the direction of the trend is clearly stated — that is, the figures are increasing.

Paragraph 4 opens with a quote from an expert, Prof. Lau. Note that he attempts to explain the trend, a common feature of this structure. ***Paragraph 7*** is a transitional paragraph that introduces another line of argument, a critique of the trend, and ***Paragraph 8*** introduces a legislative councillor who carries out the critique.

Finally, ***Paragraphs 12–13*** provide closure by returning to the focus of the original anecdote, Mr. and Mrs. Lam.

So, the *Time* trend piece is a very simple structure that can be invoked to report social indicators data in a straightforward manner that anyone can understand. With this final formula in your arsenal of news structures, you will be fully prepared for a career as a print journalist.

Appendix: Codes of Ethics

Following are two codes of ethics. The first one, promulgated by the Hong Kong Journalists Association, is Rule 19 of the association's constitution. The second one was drafted by the Society of Professional Journalists. With 12,000 members, it is the largest journalism society in America.

It should be noted that there are no enforcement provisions for either of these codes, other than the occasional letter of rebuke. It is assumed that peer pressure is enough to maintain a high standard.

Hong Kong Journalists Association
Code of Ethics

1. A journalist has a duty to maintain the highest professional and ethical standards.

2. A journalist shall at all times defend the principle of the freedom of the press and other media in relation to the collection of information and the expression of comment and criticism. He/she shall strive to eliminate distortion, news suppression and censorship.

3. A journalist shall strive to ensure that the information he/she disseminates is fair and accurate, avoid the expression of comment and conjecture as established fact and falsification by distortion, selection or misrepresentation.

4. A journalist shall rectify promptly any harmful inaccuracies, ensure that correction and apologies receive due prominence and afford the right of reply to persons criticised when the issue is of sufficient importance.

5. A journalist shall obtain information, photographs and illustrations only by straightforward means. The use of other means can be justified only by overriding considerations of the public interest. The journalist is entitled to exercise a personal conscientious objection to the use of such means.

6. Subject to justification by overriding considerations of the public interest, a journalist shall do nothing which entails intrusion into private grief and distress.

7. A journalist shall protect confidential sources of information.

8. A journalist shall not accept bribes nor shall he/she allow other inducements to influence the performance of his/her professional duties.

9. A journalist shall not lend himself/herself to the distortion or suppression of the truth because of advertising or other considerations.

10. A journalist shall not originate material which encourages discrimination on grounds of race, colour, creed, gender or sexual orientation.

11. A journalist shall not take private advantage of information gained in the course of his/her duties, before the information is public knowledge.

Society of Professional Journalists Code of Ethics

The Society of Professional Journalists believes the duty of journalists is to serve the truth.

We believe the agencies of mass communication are carriers of public discussion and information, acting on their Constitutional mandate and freedom to learn and report the facts.[1]

We believe in public enlightenment as the forerunner of justice, and in our Constitutional role to seek the truth as part of the public's right to know the truth.

We believe those responsibilities carry obligations that require journalists to perform with intelligence, objectivity, accuracy and fairness.

To these ends, we declare acceptance of the standards of practice here set forth:

I. Responsibility:

The public's right to know of events of public importance and interest is the overriding mission of the mass media. The purpose of distributing news and enlightened opinion is to serve the general welfare. Journalists who use their professional status as representatives of the public for selfish or other unworthy motives violate a high trust.

[1] "Constitutional mandate" is a reference to the First Amendment of the U.S. Constitution.

II. Freedom of the Press:

Freedom of the press is to be guarded as an inalienable right of people in a free society. It carries with it the freedom and the responsibility to discuss, question, and challenge actions and utterances of our government and of our public and private institutions. Journalists uphold the right to speak unpopular opinions and the privilege to agree with the majority.

III. Ethics:

Journalists must be free of obligation to any interest other than the public's right to know the truth.

1. Gifts, favours, free travel, special treatment or privileges can compromise the integrity of journalists and their employers. Nothing of value should be accepted.

2. Secondary employment, political involvement, holding public office, and service in community organizations should be avoided if it compromises the integrity of journalists and their employers. Journalists and their employers should conduct their personal lives in a manner that protects them from conflict of interest, real or apparent. Their responsibilities to the public are paramount. That is the nature of their profession.

3. So-called news communications from private sources should not be published or broadcast without substantiation of their claims to news values.

4. Journalists will seek news that serves the public interest, despite the obstacles. They will make constant efforts to assure that the public's business is conducted in public and that public records are open to public inspection.

5. Journalists acknowledge the newsman's ethic of protecting confidential sources of information.

6. Plagiarism is dishonest and unacceptable.

IV. Accuracy and Objectivity:

Good faith with the public is the foundation of all worthy journalism.

1. Truth is our ultimate goal.

2. Objectivity in reporting the news is another goal that serves as the mark of an experienced professional. It is a standard of performance toward which we strive. We honour those who achieve it.

3. There is no excuse for inaccuracies or lack of thoroughness.

4. Newspaper headlines should be fully warranted by the contents of the articles they accompany. Photographs and telecasts should give an accurate picture of an event and not highlight an incident out of context.

5. Sound practice makes clear distinction between news reports and expressions of opinion. News reports should be free of opinion or bias and represent all sides of an issue.

6. Partisanship in editorial comment that knowingly departs from the truth violates the spirit of American journalism.

7. Journalists recognize their responsibility for offering informed analysis, comment, and editorial opinion on public events and issues. They accept the obligation to present such material by individuals whose competence, experience, and judgment qualify them for it.

8. Special articles or presentations devoted to advocacy or the writer's own conclusions and interpretations should be labeled as such.

V. Fair Play:

Journalists at all times will show respect for the dignity, privacy, rights, and wellbeing of people encountered in the course of gathering and presenting the news.

1. The news media should not communicate unofficial charges affecting reputation or moral character without giving the accused a chance to reply.

2. The news media must guard against invading a person's right to privacy.

3. The media should not pander to morbid curiosity about details of vice and crime.

4. It is the duty of news media to make prompt and complete correction of their errors.

5. Journalists should be accountable to the public for their reports and the public should be encouraged to voice its grievances against the media. Open dialogue with our readers, viewers, and listeners should be fostered.

VI. Mutual Trust:

Adherence to this code is intended to preserve and strengthen the bond of mutual trust and respect between American journalists and American people.

The Society shall — by programmes of education and other means — encourage individual journalists to adhere to these tenets, and shall encourage journalistic publications and broadcasters to recognize their responsibility to frame codes of ethics in concert with their employees to serve as guidelines in furthering these goals.

Index